I0091915

The Social and Cultural
Order of Ancient Egypt

The Social and Cultural Order of Ancient Egypt

An Ethnographic and Regional Analysis

Steen Bergendorff

LEXINGTON BOOKS

Lanham • Boulder • New York • London

Published by Lexington Books
An imprint of The Rowman & Littlefield Publishing Group, Inc.
4501 Forbes Boulevard, Suite 200, Lanham, Maryland 20706
www.rowman.com

6 Tinworth Street, London SE11 5AL, United Kingdom

Copyright © 2020 The Rowman & Littlefield Publishing Group, Inc.

All rights reserved. No part of this book may be reproduced in any form or by any electronic or mechanical means, including information storage and retrieval systems, without written permission from the publisher, except by a reviewer who may quote passages in a review.

British Library Cataloguing in Publication Information Available

Library of Congress Cataloging-in-Publication Data Available

Names: Bergendorff, Steen, author.
Title: The social and cultural order of ancient Egypt: an ethnographic and
    regional analysis / Steen Bergendorff.
Description: Lanham: Lexington Books, 2019. | Includes bibliographical references
    and index. | Summary: "In The Social and Cultural Order of Ancient Egypt, Steen
    Bergendorff argues that ancient Egyptian culture can only be understood in relation
    to its reproductive condition and that ancient Egypt must be seen as part of a larger
    regional trade network including the Levant and Mesopotamia in the west and Nubia
    and Africa to the south"—Provided by publisher.
Identifiers: LCCN 2019045760 (print) | LCCN 2019045761 (ebook) |
    ISBN 9781793610041 (cloth) | ISBN 9781793610058 (epub)
    ISBN 9781793610065 (pbk)
Subjects: LCSH: Egypt—Civilization—To 332 B.C.
Classification: LCC DT61 .B45 2019 (print) | LCC DT61 (ebook) |
    DDC 932/.01—dc23
LC record available at https://lccn.loc.gov/2019045760
LC ebook record available at https://lccn.loc.gov/2019045761

Contents

Introduction

Ancient Egypt. It continues to challenge our imagination and it gives rise to endless speculations. There are good reasons for this interest in Ancient Egypt. It has mesmerized people all through the ages. Everything about it seems splendid and extraordinary. It was a time and place where everything seemed mythical and magical. Egypt seems full of wonders from an ancient, mysterious, and bygone world—a world of majestic buildings and seemingly strange practices.

Ancient Egypt has mesmerized people all through the ages. Even the Old Greek philosophers were confounded. Herodotus (writing at the time of the 27th Dynasty), when introducing his readers to the curious land of Egypt and her even more curious inhabitants, writes:

> About Egypt I shall have a great deal more to relate because of the number of remarkable things which the country contains, and because of the fact that more monuments which beggar description are to be found there than anywhere else in the world. . . . Not only is the Egyptian climate peculiar to that country and the Nile different in its behavior from other rivers elsewhere, but the Egyptians themselves in their manners and customs seem to have reversed the ordinary practices of mankind. (Tyldesley 2011: 16)

This fascination with Ancient Egypt seems never to have waned off. Nowadays, the same kind of enthrallment can be found in hundreds of books and on the internet, for example:

> Ancient Egypt was the preeminent civilization in the Mediterranean world. . . . Egypt's majesty has long entranced archaeologists and historians and created a vibrant field of study all its own: Egyptology. . . . The picture that emerges is of

a culture with few equals in the beauty of its art, the accomplishment of its architecture or the richness of its religious traditions. (History.com Editors 2009)

In addition, pictorial and written sources reveal nearly everything about everyday life in Ancient Egypt. Inside the tombs, every single ordinary activity is on display. Moreover, the chronicles tell us who built the different temples, when and where. It was a place of seemingly limitless richness, majestic buildings, and strange practices—Impressive Pyramids, Divine Pharaohs, and surreal Gods.

However, these drawings and chronicles are also completely silent about the rationales and dynamics that motivated the ancient Egyptians to build exceptional structures like the pyramids. There are very few records about their construction. Later civilizations, awestruck at these huge and amazing structures—the only remaining wonders of the ancient world—can find no explanation at all for them in the Egyptian records. Not a word. Indeed, "no ancient texts have been found that clearly tell us how or why pyramid complexes were built" (Wenke 2009: 296). It seems the truth about this strange culture is buried somewhere in the sand. What is more, our curiosity is kept alive as new fantastic finds keeps emerging from the ground. Dig deeper.

Alternatively, we could gather all the present archeological knowledge about Ancient Egypt's social reproduction, social organization, and cosmology to give a holistic account of its "cultural order" and then relate this to its Ancient practices. Pyramids, Pharaohs, and local Gods are all cultural constructs.

Therefore, our understanding of all these wonders and strange practices of Ancient Egypt have to be supplemented by a new narrative based on a holistic ethnographic perspective that relate all these phenomena to its social organization and culture. Hence, the contention of this book is that all these wonders and the social organization that made them possible can only be understood by a holistic ethnographic study. In short, we need to understand Ancient Egyptian culture.

To help in this endeavor, we are so lucky that pictorial and written sources reveal nearly everything about everyday life in Ancient Egypt. Inside the tombs, every single ordinary activity is on display. Therefore, our understanding of all these wonders and strange practices of Ancient Egypt have to be supplemented by a new narrative based on a holistic ethnographic perspective that relate all these phenomena to its social organization and culture. Hence, the contention of this book is that all these wonders and the social organization that made them possible can only be understood by a holistic ethnographic study. In short, we need to understand Ancient Egyptian culture.

To recreate Egypt's ancient cultural order, we need anthropological theory and ethnographic material to complement and enhance the archeological material. To be sure, anthropology is not a monolithic science. There are all kinds of theories. To specify the anthropological legacy of this study: culture is not seen as something people have, but as something they do (to make sense of, and negotiate, the constitution of their social world). As such, Egyptian culture is not regarded as possessing inherent qualities, or as a self-contained island characterized by particular traits.

Instead, culture is here seen as linked to, or embedded in, a particular form of social organization that, in turn, is linked to larger systems of reproduction that condition the nature and possibilities of the social system in question. In Friedman's worlds:

> Our practical life is embedded in our material existences, which are themselves constituted within social reproductive processes. (Friedman 2014)

As is evident, this way of understanding culture means that culture and its cosmology and categories are embedded in the reproductive condition of the groups involved. These "materialistic" conditions define what cannot be done (symbolically), but not how it is done. Otherwise, people would merely live in a fantasy world—and to be sure, for some it appears that the Ancient Egyptians really did so. They did not.

To undersand Egypt's Divine kingship, enormous buildings, and wonders of the world and why these phenomena was initially located in a particular location on the Nile, Egyptian history needs to be inserted into a regional perspective (parce Bergendorff 1996, Wallerstein 1974, Friedman 1994, Frank 1998).

This theoretical model about regional reproduction simply states that the economic sphere is always larger than its corresponding cultural order, but that the economic sphere produces social conditions that local people have a condition—the resultant negotiated order is what we call culture. It is therefore important to establish the reproductive condition from the earliest times of Ancient Egypt, their locations and their relations to the larger world.

This approach to Ancient Egypt offer an explanation for its practices and cultural order and the marvelous constructions they made as well as the dynamics that made this possible. In other words, the aim here is to understand how Ancient Egyptian cosmology and practice produced a social world that made all these marvels and wonders possible, but which also produced a very hierarchical society.

Therefore, we first need to place Ancient Egypt in the regional perspective that supplied the material conditions for its reproduction. Then we need to investigate into how these material conditions were socially organized, which in all pre-monetary societies are done by some kind of kinship system.

Then Ancient social condition and its resultant organization has to be related to its cosmology, that is, its worldview that account for the forces that the Ancient believed "moved" the surrounding world. Such worldview finds its expression in, for example, stories about genesis and in concepts of personhood.

We know that what was to become Ancient Egypt started in around 4000 BC with the Badarians. These people were herders who circulated between the Eastern Desert and the Nile alluvium on a seasonal basis according to available resources. Badarian culture changed into what is known as the Naqada people. Due to climate change, the Naqadans gradually moved toward the river alluvial. Over the years, Naqada society became increasingly hierarchical.

Then there were initially three centers of Ancient development with social differentiation and hierarchy. They were all located in Upper Egypt (to the south); Naqada, Abydos, and Hierakonpolis (later to be part of the same political unity probably ruled by a person called Narmer). Significantly, all these centers were located close to large gold deposits in the Eastern Desert, and tellingly the ancient name for Naqada was Nubt, the Egyptian word for gold. Nothing remotely similar transpired in Lower Egypt (to the north).

So social development started with groups of herders long before Ancient Egypt became known as a breadbasket (later used by the Romans), and this development seems closely linked to the gold deposits in the Eastern Desert. Actually, Ancient Egypt is the only known supplier of gold to the Levant and Mesopotamia at the time. Places were gold were in large demand.

Ancient Egypt and its initial development therefore seem closely associated with the gold deposits in the Eastern Desert. The utilization of this sought-after resource in the Levant and Mesopotamia linked Egypt to the larger world. Gold therefore seem to be a major factor in the materialistic condition of the development of Ancient Egypt. It therefore also seems probably that gold and its monopolization by smaller groups determined the relationship between groups inside Ancient Egypt.

In non-monetarized societies, relationships between groups are negotiated through some form of kinship system. Kinship is the primordial way of organizing resources between groups and it reflects the character of the social reproduction of a society. Therefore, it is exchange and alliance relations that determines the kind of kinship system a society has. Kinship is a way of distributing resources between groups (Bergendorff 2016). Ancient Egypt and its resource distribution must therefore be expressed through some form of kinship system.

Moreover, there are a limited number of kinship systems. But all systems form essential parts of a social organization, and therefore kinship systems are also a basic symbolic way of expressing the resource situation of a given society. By comparing ethnographic material with ancient practices, we can determine what kind of kinship system were likely to have operated in

Ancient Egypt. This, on the other hand, would also explain some Ancient practices, such as Divine Kinship and sibling marriage.

Seen in this way, the Pharaoh's position is a result of the resource distribution in society and an accompanying kinship system. Gold would be an essential part of such a kinship system. In a preliminary way, we can establish that the observed practices in Ancient Egypt points to some form of a *matrilateral cross-cousin marriage (with avuncular residence)* (more later).

The resulting reality was symbolically negotiated in the form of a cosmology and a conception of genesis and the constitution of the world. This was a double-sided world, as also known from ethnographic material, with a sphere for the living and one for the dead, both equally important for the individual. In a way, everybody lived in both worlds simultaneously, with a part in the world of the ancestors and one among the living, an unseen world and a visible world. Such a worldview goes a long way in explaining many Ancient practices. Pharaohs being special cases were thought to be able to live simultaneously in both realms of existence, by their direct genealogical connection to the first ancestors and the creator of the world.

Living in such a world was equally reflected in the ancient conception of personhood. This consisted in several aspects or personalities, called the *ba*, the *ka*, and the *ank* all "housed" in the visible realm in a "body." With the help of ethnographic material, these aspects of personhood have to be related to each other and to the larger cosmology.

After having established the character of and relationship between these (often presented as disparate) cultural elements, we can move forward to explain Ancient practices such as the Narmer Palette, large enclosures, the so-called *sed*-festival, Pharaoh's double crowns, their titles and the purpose for building pyramids.

Chapter 1

A Regional Perspective on Ancient Egypt

Ancient Egypt became known as the breadbasket of the Roman Empire. It therefore seems that its fertile landscape had to be a major factor in its road to glory and splendor. It is for instance often assumed that already by Badarian time this agricultural potential was the prime motor in Ancient Egypt's initial development.

However, such an agricultural potential potential for creating civilizations has long since been disputed in anthropology. There seems to be other factors involved. Otherwise, it remains a conundrum to explain why the Badarian/Naqada geographical location was so prone to producing highly unequal societies with extreme status differences between the rulers and the populace.

This development is either explained as the result of charismatic persons who were able to enthrall their populations and use their power to subdue adjacent populaces, or is simply explained as a result of the fertile river plain and its nearly unlimited potential for agricultural production, which many Egyptologists claim that an emergent elite managed to gain control over, becoming immensely rich in the process.

Frankfort, one of the early Egyptologists, represent an early version of the first explanation. He thinks that there was a basic cultural unity in the Nile valley. According to him, such a unity must have been a contribution factor to the sudden efflorescence of culture under the First Dynasty. Continuing:

> Within such a conglomerate of small communities, larger political units may originate . . . paramount chiefs may arise, when a strong man or war leader begins to extend his power beyond his own group. (Frankfort 1978 [1948]: 16–17)

More recently, Raffaele gives the following explanation for the efflorescence of Ancient Egypt:

> Initially, these "elites" lived in small villages sparsely scattered along the Nile valley, which was not very densely populated at that time; but the climatic conditions ceased to be favorable for a life far from the river, hence a small population began to concentrate nearer to the Nile river. . . . Once a group of individuals took control of a larger population (due to charisma, success in battle, superstitious reasons, inclination to power or other attributes perceived as proper for a leader), this group came to constitute the ruling class, while the remainder became the ruled. . . . The rulers exploited the subjected classes who were forced to produce for them. (Raffaele 2003: 102)

In a very short version, the emergence of leaders is just explained as a "need" of the ancient Egyptians:

> From early times on, the Egyptians believed that they needed a spiritual leader who could treat with the dangerous world of the gods on behalf of humanity. (Pinch 2004: 4)

However, these processes did not occur in the Lower Egyptian Delta, which had a similar material culture and an equal potential, at least, for agricultural production. Such explanations about social evolution and the establishment of social hierarchy is, as Ekholm Friedman rightly points out,

> to avoid the problem that surplus grain cannot be locally transformed into bronze, cloth, palaces (of imported stone), fine jewelry, and weapons—hallmarks of the great civilization. (Ekholm Friedman 2008: 143)

Furthermore, there are no social dynamics at play at all in these versions of events. There are no incentives for unequal exchange, which is at the root of social differentiation. This lack of incentives is known as "the peasant enigma," referred to by Karl Marx as

> "the peasant sack of potatoes." Peasant society is "formed by simple addition of homologous magnitudes, much as potatoes in a sack form a sack of potatoes." (Marx and Engels 1852: 338)

All these similar social farming units or "potatoes in a sack" would have no incentives to produce a surplus and start exchanging in order to create status hierarchies. Everybody in these situations would have been able to produce for his or her own needs. Subsistence farmers simply do not produce a surplus that can be appropriated: not by fraud, not by force, not by conspiracy.

Subsistence farmers traditionally grow most of what they eat, build the houses they live in from local materials, and make the clothes they wear independently from the marketplace. (Ethnography.com 2016)

We must search for some other social dynamic that could have produced the social hierarchies that existed in Badarian and Naqada societies, compared to the Delta societies where they seemingly did not exist. These issues can only be grasped in relation to the reproductive conditions, that is, Ancient Egypt's position and role in the larger world with which they had important exchange and trading relations.

Accordingly, we first have to insert Ancient Egypt into its proper regional context and to discern how this produced different life conditions in Upper and Lower Egypt. The short answer to this question is *gold*. This was the foundation of the Egyptian prestige economy throughout the ages. Gold was the predominant product that linked Egypt to their surrounding world. Gold made it possible to import large quantities of prestige goods. Gold was the element that differentiated Upper Egypt from Lower Egypt and made the pharaohs tremendously rich.

The task here is, therefore, to search the Egyptian archeological record for issues connected to its material reproduction and wholly concerned with establishing Ancient Egypt's relationships with the surrounding world through its different epochs.

BADARIAN ERA

What was to become Ancient Egypt started around 4500 years BC with the so-called Badarian Culture (named after the present location of major finds from this period) that began to flourish in middle Egypt. Badarian sites also existed in the Eastern Desert in the Wadi Hammamat, the Wadi Atulla, and Ras Samadi (Lloyd 2014: 36) (*wadis* being dried up riverbeds running into the Nile).

From recent excavations, we know that the Badarians moved up and down the Nile valley and into the surrounding deserts, and they appear to have travelled with their herds onto the dry plains above the valley cliffs (Romer 2013: 45). They were mobile herding groups (Wengrow 2009: 27) who were well acquainted with what was to become the Eastern Desert, which they used as grassland for their cattle. Otherwise, they lived in transitory structures, "sticks and matting appearing to have served as the main materials for human shelter" (Romer 2013: 46).

The difference between valley and desert was less marked at that time, and the contents of Badarian burials are testimony to the extraction and circulation of mineral and metal resources from the Eastern Desert (Wengrow 2009: 54). Moreover, "the sheer quantity of desert resources in valley cemeteries suggests the existence of regular networks of procurement and exchange throughout the fifth millennium" (Wengrow 2006: 54). Graves and grave goods have also been found in the Eastern Desert along the Wadi Hammamat and the Wadi Atulla, and a tumulus burial containing a gold-wire bracelet has been found in Wadi Elei in the eastern desert of Lower Nubia. As Wadi Hammamat is one of the major gold deposit sites in Egypt, this strongly indicates that the Badarians used the desert not only as grazing land but also for gold prospecting.

Grave goods from that time are abundant; they are often rich, and they show differences in wealth, providing evidence of early social stratification. It seems that products from Near Eastern sources were of great importance, probably being used as prestige goods and markers of social status (Lloyd 2014: 37). Such large quantities of imported materials indicate that the Badarians were involved in a well-developed trade network (Mark 2006: 12). And there is at least one documented trade route running north-eastwards out of Egypt, skirting Sinai, and climbing up the coastline of the eastern Mediterranean (Rice 1993: 37).

In Lower Egypt, what is today called North Egypt, we see a different kind of development. Here we find the Merimde people who were farmers and herders. They were involved in trade with Palestine where the Ghassulian group was evolving. Ghassulians had extensive trade networks involving obsidian from Anatolia, possible arsenical copper also from Anatolia, Iran, or the Caucasus mountains, shells from the Red Sea, and elephant tusks from Egypt and North Syria (Mark 2006: 14). Moreover, metallurgical technology, wall paintings, and mace heads linked the Ghassulians to Mesopotamia and thereby at least indirectly connected the Mesopotamians to Egypt (Mark 2006: 14).

Further developments in Palestine seem to have intensified trade connections. In Mesopotamia, the so-called Early Uruk period (ca. 3900–3600 BC) was followed by the Middle and Late Uruk periods (ca. 3600–3200/3100) (Algaze 2014: 14). These were periods in which Mesopotamian imports were impressive, encompassing a huge variety of products, especially gold for jewelry (Algaze 2014: 95), showing that there was an increasing demand for gold in the Middle East.

By the early-mid fourth millennium BC, a few larger cities emerged in the Middle East. As Wengrow writes,

[A]t a number sites, administrative practices—involving the use of seals to manage and record the flow of people and goods—were concentrated within a small number of buildings, distinguished by their monumental size and public function. (Wengrow 2006: 36)

In the mid-fourth millennium one of these administrative centers, Tell Brak, had expanded to a hundred hectares in size, harboring a centralized management of resources using elaborate pot-marks, tokens, and also numerical and pictographic notations (Wengrow 2006: 37).

In the early fourth millennium, cross-cultural interaction also intensified along the Mediterranean, and its impact was felt from southeastern Turkey to Lower Egypt. In addition, Levantine vessel forms strongly influenced ceramic production at the Lower Egyptian site of Maadi (Wengrow 2009: 34–35). These changes in the Levant and Mesopotamia also signaled a change in Egypt. From now on, North and South Egypt followed different social trajectories. In the South, the Naqada I, II, III sequence developed, and in the north Maadi the Butho culture emerged.

NAQADA ERA

The transition from Badarian to Naqada I (or the Amaratian period from ca. 4000–3500 BC) was not a sudden cultural break but consisted of slow changes and a shift in prime location (Midant-Reynes 2000: 185). Badarian ephemeral huts and temporary encampments during seasonal exploitation of pastureland gave way to more permanent houses, for instance at Hierakonpolis (Midant-Raynes 2000: 185). The Naqada (also named after the present location of major finds) raised various domesticated species such as goats, sheep, bovid, and pigs. They grew barley and wheat and perhaps also peas and vetch (Midant-Raynes 2000: 185)—indicating that there was presumably an incipient division of labor, with some herders and some cultivators. There was a growing tendency for a few individuals to be buried in tombs that were increasingly large and equipped with ever richer and more abundant grave goods (Midant-Raynes 2000: 187), suggesting that Badarian society grew richer but also more stratified.

Curiously, there is evidence in some graves of the dismemberment of bodies before burial, the purpose of which is unclear but which made it possible to bury body parts in different sites (Lloyd 2014: 46). This might very well have been the initial practice that later resurfaced in the story about the King of the so-called Netherworld, Osiris, who was dismembered by his brother Seth only to be reassembled by his sister/wife with whom he then had a son called Horus.

Foreign influence is clearly discernible in this phase of Egyptian history. As Rice writes,

> Naqada I pottery reveals some evidence of western Asiatic influence at work on what had already become basic Egyptian forms. . . . There are similarities with some designs developed in south-western Asia. (Rice 1991: 31)

Naqada settlements extend from Hierakonpolis in the south to Matmar in the north, with a concentration of important Naqada I sites along the river between Abydos and Naqada (Rice 1991: 31). From the later part of the period, Naqada I pottery, palettes, combs, and hairpins have been found in early A-Group graves in Lower Nubia (Mark 2006: 14–15). These finds link the Nile valley to Palestine in the north and to Nubia in the south in one long stretch of trade and cultural interchanges.

Naqada culture had three main centers: Naqada itself, being the modern location of the place the Egyptians called Nubt; Hierakonpolis, being the Greek name for Nekhen, the place of the falcon; and Abydos (This). All three sites are located near wadi-entrances to the Eastern Desert and major gold deposits. Tellingly, Nubt is the ancient Egyptian word for gold. Likewise, the A-group in Nubia was located close to a wadi leading to gold deposits. Moreover, in all these places rock art began to appear on the cliffs in the wadis, and was concentrated on routes to the gold mines (Lankester 2013: 27)—perhaps to mark (clan)ownership.

These Naqada locations were essential to the evolution of Ancient Egypt. It was in these places that Egyptian culture started to flourish. Not all places along the Nile experienced the same pace of economic development, which was always differentiated in Egypt, with some places like Middle Egypt hardly participating at all in the momentous changes (Wilkinson 2006: 45) that occurred in Naqada, Hierakonpolis, and Abydos. Social change seems to have come to those who had the gold, while the rest lived in the quieter backwaters (Wilkinson 2006: 45).

Contemporaneously with Naqada I, Maadi became an important trading hub in the north, located on the east side of the Nile just south of the Delta (Wilkinson 2003: 126). Their farming methods were similar to those of early Naqadans. They made very distinctive small vases of basalt that have been found in graves and settlements up and down the Nile Valley (Romer 2013: 100). As Wilkinson writes, the Maadis lived off trade.

> Behind the village, the Wadi Digla led eastward towards the Great Bitter Lakes, the Gulf of Suez, onward to the Sinai peninsula and Palestine beyond. (Wilkinson 2003: 126)

The Maadis' "fame" was due to their position on a major trading route to Palestine. They probably imported a great deal of different products from Palestine and beyond, but little evidence for the exact nature of this trade survives except for the carrying pots themselves (Romer 2013: 101). Some of the first stone buildings found in Egypt were also located in Maadi. These were similar to buildings found in south Levant, and a great deal of Levantine pottery was also found at Maadi (Romer 2013: 100). The Maadi were clearly also in contact with the southern Naqada, judging from the appearance of their slate palettes, disc-shaped mace-heads, jars of diorite and black-topped pottery (Mark 2006: 16).

Around 3500 BC, Maadi and Buto were flourishing trading and farming communities but, contrary to the situation in Upper Egypt, there is little evidence of any significant status differentiation in terms of inherited access to wealth, power, and prestige (Wenke 2009: 205). Although heavily involved in trade with the Levant, Maadi's buildings and graves only reflect minor differences in social rank and wealth differentials—nothing like the contemporary sites in the south. Maadi apparently never saw an elite emerge to exploit its trading position (Wenke 2009: 227).

Contemporaneously, larger urban sites developed in North Mesopotamia. This also affected Tell Brak, which became one of the largest sites in (present-day) Syria. Here we find the famous Eye Temple that had recessed and buttressed main walls, a decoration system that later became the trademark of status graves in Egypt. In this

> "temple" there was a "most remarkable altar" decorated to represent the façade of a building, perhaps that of the temple itself. The altar is made up of blue limestone, white marble and corrugated green shale all set in a frame covered in gold foil and held in place with silver nails. (Crawford 2004: 122)

If nothing else, these examples show that gold was in high demand throughout the Middle East. In this area, the elite evidently had a predilection for gold.

As time went on, the Tepe Gawa site was also becoming more prosperous and more hierarchical. We see a significant quantity of gold appearing in its tombs, together with other exotic materials such as lapis that came from Badakhshan, turquoise from Iran and obsidian probably from Anatolia (Crawford 2004: 139), indicating a very wide and diversified trade network linking Egypt to the Levant and Mesopotamia and onward to Afghanistan and India. Gold seems to have been the Egyptian contribution to this network.

We see a growing interaction between regions at this time, a situation that is reflected in the presence of small, but consistent quantities of lapis lazuli in Upper Egyptian graves. Finished items of Mesopotamian or Iranian origin, such as cylinder stamp seals, also appear (Wengrow 2006: 40). The whole scale of Egyptian interaction with the Middle East was also transformed at this time by the establishment of a pack-donkey route crossing the Nile delta to southern Israel across northern Sinai. New products found their way to Egypt, such as wine, resin, and olive oil (Wengrow 2006: 40).

These developments are generally characterized as the transition to Naqada II or Gerzean, which are in turn usually divided into an early phase (ca.

3500–3300 BC), and a late phase (ca. 3300–3200 BC) (Mark 2006: 18). This shift in denomination is mostly based on a change in pottery style (Wengrow 2006: 94), and to a certain extent also in domestic architecture (Wenke 2009: 216), and in the elaboration of graves in Upper Egypt.

Throughout Egypt, regional pottery manufacturing traditions were replaced by a single uniform technique, which used straw in lieu of local varieties of temper. This new way of producing pottery was followed by a marked increase in the amount of vessels produced. In contrast to the Naqada I period, these vessels were deposited in large quantities in graves. At the same time, this shift in pottery style indicated a shift in dietary habits. Both in Mesopotamia and Egypt, the change reflects a centralization in the production of bread and beer (Wengrow 2006: 94). According to Wengrow, the adoption of fermented cereal products in Egypt might be viewed as a further appropriation of prestige technologies from the outside. He also argues that this implies a more direct form of contact between Egypt and Mesopotamia, in contrast to other forms of prestige goods that could travel in long distance relay exchange systems (Wengrow 2006: 96–97).

In Upper and Middle Egypt, the pit houses were abandoned and people began to live in mud-brick houses composed of rectangular rooms (Wenke 2009: 216). Together with the dietary modifications and the centralized production of pottery, this change in housing preferences suggests a shift toward a more sedentary lifestyle. In general, quantity production of trade goods increased in this period, and graves became relatively large and contained goods such as stone mace-heads and painted vessels (Wenke 2009: 222).

Graves in this period indicate a society with greater wealth, division of labor, and social stratification. By the end of the Naqada II period, burials for the elite had evolved into larger brick-lined chambers, some with more rooms and richer offerings (Mark 2006: 18–19). The three larger settlements in Upper Egypt showed considerable progress in urbanization. In addition, Naqada contained a large enclosure, which Lloyd declared to be indisputably a major ceremonial center. Finds suggest that it was consecrated to the major deity, Horus (Lloyd 2014: 45), indicating an emergent status hierarchy, Horus being the paramount deity in Egyptian Kingship.

Parallel to the Naqada sequence in Egypt, a similar development took place in Lower Nubia. Here the emerging society is called the A-group. The Nubian sequence mirrors the Naqada sequence. In Nubia, the different periods are called Early, Classic, and Terminal, the latter being called Terminal since the A-group seems to have disappeared with the onset of the First Dynasty in Egypt. Like its contemporaries Naqada (Nubt), Hierakonpolis (Nekhen) and Abydos (This) in Egypt, this group was also located close to major gold deposits in the Eastern Desert. To all intents and purposes, these four locations may have been the local motors of Egyptian developments in

Pre-dynastic times. As Wilkinson writes, "The Nubian valley was essentially a continuation of the Egyptian Nile valley" (2006: 175). There was also considerable exchange between these locations (Shinnie 1996: 44).

Meanwhile, Mesopotamia kept on developing, and increasing its trading potential, with an ever-expanding demand for gold. Rice has put forward a theory that Mesopotamians' search for gold could or would have brought them into contact with the Valley people. Such contact could also have occasioned an influx of specialists and artisans into Egypt (Rice1993: 35), drawn toward the independent "courts" that were established at this time in Hierakonpolis, Naqada, and Abydos. The names of these early "kings" have been found recorded on the rocks of southern Upper Egypt, but are not easily decipherable (Rice 1993: 36). It is, however, clear that these "courts" controlled trade and access to the gold reserves, and thus, "[i]t would have been to their courts that the gold-hungry easterners made their way" (Rice 1993: 36).

In the same period, the city-states of southern Mesopotamia began to extend their maritime interests into the Persian Gulf (Wengrow 2006: 142). Maadi lost its importance and most of the settlements disappeared. It seems that the donkey route to Palestine was abandoned. Instead, the coastal settlement of Buto grew in importance, and new settlements such as Minshat Abu Omar sprang up closer to the sea (Mark 2006: 19). This signaled a change from overland routes traversed by pack animals to sea-born cargo ships, which seems to have vastly increased the capacity for long distance trade in exotics. As Wengrow writes,

> [V]ia this route, groups [presumably with access to local commodities such as gold] maintained access to small quantities of crafted foods and exotic materials deriving from lowland Mesopotamia/Iran and the Fertile Crescent. (2006: 140)

Though perhaps not in such small quantities after all, Egypt's relationships both with Palestine and Nubia during this period continued to intensify (Mark 2006: 21).

Both parties in the trading network—Egypt/Nubia and Mesopotamia—needed prestige goods in ever-larger quantities. Prestige goods are essential in status formation and in the accompanying political struggles for power. This is what we see playing out most vividly in Upper Egypt during the period in question. As a result of the new opportunities for long-distance trade and the changes it brought to Egypt, the elites in Upper Egypt began to consolidate their control over nearby metal and mineral resources, leading to a major restructuring of the local economy (Wengrow 2006: 142).

This marked the beginning of what has been called Naqada III, or Dynasty 0 (ca. 3200–3100 BC). It brought about major changes in Upper Egypt which were so drastic, and seemed to spell such a complete break with the past, that Flinders Petrie thought they were caused by an invasion from the east by a "dynastic race" that triggered Egypt's sudden quantum shift in social complexity. He did not consider that the Egyptians themselves were able to accomplish such a "level of true civilization" (Midant-Reynes 2002: 31).

Some immediate results of the increase in trade made possible by the new maritime route included the simplification or impoverishment of everyday material culture, and a marked increase in inequality in Upper Egypt. Concurrently, we see a specialization and monopolization of artistic expression within so-called elite circles and an impoverishment of everyday products. This impoverishment is particularly obvious in grave goods and in the ceramic repertoire. At the cemetery of el-Kab, fifty graves have been excavated from this period. In contrast to the more sumptuous graves of Abydos pertaining to the emergent rulers, these cemeteries are "low-status" graves. Nevertheless, they show clear changes in material culture.

Objects found in these graves are not decorated; objects used for personal adornment that were formerly widespread are no longer in evidence, and cosmetic palettes are now mostly plain (Wengrow 2006: 155). Simultaneously, there are some pronounced changes in the ceramic repertoire. Ceramics no longer have figural paintings as in the previous period, and pottery as a whole shows a greater degree of homogeneity and repetition (Wengrow 2006: 156). The scale of coarse ware production throughout Egypt shows a marked increase that is also evident in the Nile delta at Buto, for instance (Wengrow 2006: 156). These shifts indicate a move toward mass production that is consistent with a vast increase in trade.

Paradoxically, most of the evidence about life in Egypt comes from the dead, therefore graves and burials have become our most significant source of information about social life and development in the region. The graves offer us a glimpse of the marked inequality that appeared in the Naqada III period. Already in the Naqada II period, the wealthy in Naqada (Nubt/gold), or what is often termed the ruling or exploiting class, were increasingly differentiating themselves from the general population. They had separate cemeteries, some with large brick-lined tombs furnished with abundant grave goods (Wilkinson 2006: 37). Wilkinson writes that the splendor and size of their burials suggest that some individuals controlled larger territories that he finds amount to "kingdoms" (Wilkinson 2006: 37).

Hierakonpolis now covered an area that exceeded any other contemporary settlements. It also benefited from access to gold deposits in the eastern desert. Close by the main "city," we find extensive cemeteries and a concentration of so-called elite burials in one cemetery (Wilkinson 2006: 38). At Abydos, the third center of Naqada "culture," we find some of largest and most complex graves. In the so-called "cemetery U" from the early Naqada III period, tomb U-j is the largest, having twelve chambers. It provides evidence of the use of an early form of hieroglyphic script for record keeping and commemoration purposes (Lloyd 2014: 49).

In tomb U-j, dozens of inscribed bone labels were found that if they could be translated could identified the content and localities of the products kept in the grave. (Wilkinson 2006: 41). The owner of tomb U-j certainly engaged in large-scale trade with the Near East, since the tomb contained over 400 imported vessels from Syria-Palestine. These probably contained wine, and the sheer number of pots illustrates the scale of trade between Upper Egypt passing through Lower Egypt and on to the Near East (Wilkinson 2006: 41). It has been estimated that the tomb may have contained as many as seven hundreds of these bottles amounting to up to 4.5 liters of wine (Wengrow 2006: 202).

These goods clearly suggest that trade or exchange between Upper and Lower Egypt was large scale and to some extent formalized. And herein lies the conundrum. Wilkinson "do[es] not know what Egyptian products passed in the other direction" (Wilkinson 2006: 41). Judging from the locations of these Upper Egyptian settlements, an informed guess would be gold. Then again, Wilkinson is not entirely sure: although he thinks that the Egyptians' share in their trading relationship with the Near East is less well attested, he writes that gold may have been an important export for Pre-dynastic Egypt and that it was highly valued throughout the ancient world (Wilkinson 2006: 43).

At the same time, Lower Nubia was also experiencing massive changes and increasing inequality and exploitation benefiting only a small segment of society. Nubia was also a main exporter of gold. At this time, the graves of the Terminal A-group contain large quantities of imported Egyptian artifacts, indicating intense trade between Upper Egypt and Lower Nubia (Wilkinson 2006: 177).

There are other Nubian affinities with Upper Egypt. At what has been called the royal cemetery at Qustul in Lower Nubia, excavators found a decorated incense burner featuring many different motives, among others "the ruler" wearing a so-called crown that was thought to represent and be used by Upper Egyptian "kings." At the very least, this suggests a relationship between the two places in terms of their representations or pictorial depictions of their rulers. It is, however, a misnomer seen in relation to the standard interpretation of "crowns" as indicating a "uniting of the two lands." This "crown" seems to have been on a walkabout.

Back in Egypt (which is essentially a contemporary division of a once continuous territory) the political landscape was changing. Up until this time, the three centers in Upper Egypt seem to have evolved in unity and in parallel. This changed, as is depicted in a rock carving at Gebel Tjauti in the hills near Abydos. This is the first found example of a carving that seems to tell a story.

It is interpreted as depicting a triumphal procession of King Scorpion, after his troops had conquered the rival king and town of Naqada (Nubt/gold). The carving features an image of a falcon incised above an image of a scorpion, and is therefore interpreted as the name of a "king" because the falcon was used as a symbol for "divine kingship" throughout Egyptian history (Wenke 2009: 229).

This is not idle speculation. Such an annexation of Naqada seems to be supported by a gap in the sequence of élite burials at Naqada, whereas the same period is marked by ever larger tombs at Hierakonpolis at what has been termed Locality 6 (Wilkinson 2006: 50). It seems that at around 3200 BC, Hierakonpolis had become the capital (if such a word can be used) of southern Egypt. At Hierakonpolis there was also built a large cobblestone foundation that has been interpreted as a fortified palace, temple, or administrative center (Wenke 2009: 223). At Abydos, the already mentioned tomb U-j shows that this city was already dominant at the time (Wilkinson 2006: 50).

Consequently, there were only two centers left in Upper Egypt: Hierakonpolis/Nekhen and Abydos/This, Hierakonpolis being the southernmost town with access to Nubia and greater Africa and Abydos/This the northernmost town with trade routes running to the Far East via Buto. In Hierakonpolis, "King" Scorpion reigned, and as Wilkinson suggests he may have been at least partly contemporary with "King" Narmer at This/Abydos (Wilkinson 2006: 57).

You would think that "King" Scorpion would have had the upper hand by now after having annexed Naqada (Nubt), but in the end it was the Abydos/This "Kings" who managed to annex Hierakonpolis. Being located to the north of Hierakonpolis, Abydos/This had a strategic advantageous position in relationship to the all-important trade route to the Levant and Mesopotamia, which ran down river via Buto. Hierakonpolis traders had to pass by Abydos. Not a favorable situation.

Most probably, Narmer achieved this annexation. He is the most prominent figure in the archeological record from this period. Up until this point, the gold deposits of Upper Egypt had sustained three "royal" families, but now they sustained only one family. If that is true, it means that Narmer would have controlled all of Upper Egypt's gold deposits, making him the world's wealthiest man at the time. Narmer seems to have used his wealth to establish ever wider trade connections and he seems to have been a very keen explorer. His name is attested in several places in Upper and Lower Egypt, in the Eastern Desert, and in the Near East (Lloyd 2014: 60).

At this point in Ancient Egyptian history there are some doubt as to what transpired and who was responsible, that is, if there was a unification of the "two lands" Upper and Lower Egypt and by whom. Narmer is the major contender in uniting "The Two Lands" but also a man called Menes is considered because on later king lists he appear as the one who accomplished such a feat due to his double titles.

One reason for favoring Narmer is a palette found in the Hierakonpolis cache. It is the first artefact that bears the name of a "king" inscribed in a *serekh* frame. Midant-Reynes simply states that this palette is

the first evidence for the unification of the two lands' and that its message is crystal clear, i.e. that "the king has defeated the Delta enemy." (Mident-Reynes 2000: 243)

Narmer appears on both sides of the palette. On one side, Narmer is the main figure, who is pictured holding an instrument in his right hand, believed to be a mace, but, curiously, he is holding the handle in the middle. In the other hand, which rests on the head of a kneeling man, he grasps a square object that resembles a box. This is interpreted as Narmer smiting the enemy. On this side of the palette, Narmer is wearing a kind of pointed headgear.

On the other side of the palette, Narmer plays a lesser role—he is pictured walking in a procession towards some slain, decapitated persons above whom there is a ship and a falcon heading towards a gate—which is interpreted as "The Gate of Horus." On this side, he is wearing a kind of pointed headgear with a curl at the front. In the middle, and taking up most space, are two entwined long-necked leopard-like creatures held in leashes by two men with significantly different appearances. This leopard-like creature is inspired by Mesopotamian iconography (Lloyd 2014: 52). Lloyd thinks that this "figure" can plausibly be interpreted as a symbol of unification. We are not informed why such a unification should have been rendered using Mesopotamian symbolism, and there is no clue as to the nature of Narmer's relationship with Mesopotamia.

Moreover, archeological excavations testify to the existence of Narmer. In 1985, the cemetery at Umm el-Qaab was re-excavated by a German expedition. Here, archeologists found an important seal impression displaying the names of rulers, beginning with Narmer and followed by Aha, Djer, Djet, Den, and the king's mother Merneith.

Another such a list was found some years later. It also listed these names as well as others until King Qa-a, the last This/Thinite kings who ended the First dynasty (Raffaele 2003: 107). This Egyptian concern with ancestry is based on a belief that (as we know from anthropology) the eldest line is more directly connected to the remote ancestors from whom all power emanates, and is therefore the ruler.

On much later king lists Narmer disappears, and instead the funerary king list at Abydos and the Royal Canon of Turin at the time of Ramses II mentions someone called Menes who is proclaimed to be the founder of Egypt

(Raffaele 2003: 107). Frankfort for instance thinks that we cannot form an adequate idea of the nature of the kingship in Egypt without a detailed knowledge of the reference to and the role played by the Royal Ancestors, and this surely involves extensive references to Menes (Meni) (1978 [1948]: 89).

Frankfort finds support for the role of Menes in a relief from the time of Ramses II. It shows a great procession of the Harvest Festival of Min. Here, statues of ancestors identified by their names are carried before the king. They include Menes as the oldest of the series (Frankfort (1978 [1948]: 89). A text accompany the pictures; make explicit the function of the statues:

> The statues of the kings of Upper and Lower Egypt [interpretation that is probably based on his title *nswt-bity*], which goes before this venerable god, Min-Kamutef, give life to King Ramses III. (Frankfort 1978 [1948]: 89)

Both the Turin Royal Canon (probably composed during the reign of Ramesses II c. 1250 BC) and the Abydos king list (from the mortuary temple of Seti, c. 1280 BC) seems to confirm the existence of Menes. Both lists start with a king named Menes (Meni). Besides his name (and all following "kings") is the title *nswt-bíty*, rendered as a sedge plant and a bee (which is often translated as "dual kings" of Upper and Lower Egypt).

To take account of later king lists Menes is explained as a substitute name for Narmer, who is proclaimed as:

> The first king of the First Dynasty was the archaeologically attested Narmer. The name Meni, "He who endures," is probably a descriptive epithet for the long lost name of the legendary king who united the Two Lands. (Pharaoh.se 2018)

However, as we have seen, "king" lists from the time of Den and Qa'a, do not mention anyone called Menes. Den's list starts with Narmer, followed by Aha, Djer, Djet, Den, and (Queen) Mermeith. Qa'a's list also starts with Narmer, followed by Aha, Djer, Wadj, Den, Anedjep, Semerket, and Qaa.

Menes is notoriously absent in these contemporary lists. Something crept in between the rule of Narmer and Den from the First Dynasty, and the later king Ramses and Seti from the 19th Dynasty. As Frankfort points out, this use of statues to represent predecessors is not observed before the New Kingdom (Frankfort 1978 [1948]: 89). There seem to have been a long time to tamper with the Royal genealogy.

A plausible explanation for the appearance of Menes is that he was inserted into the king list by some later usurper. It would not be the first time that a usurper changed the order of a genealogy to suit his claim to power. Present political might is often the most important issue in determining the genealogical order of families and ancestors. Of course, it becomes more difficult to tamper with the order of ancestors when the genealogy is written in stone, as was the case with the later lists (not the Turin Royal Canon that was written on papyrus). To this day, we do not know who made the substitution.

We do know of several examples of non-royal pretenders claiming the throne. In ca. 1319 a soldier named Horemheb who had served under Akhenatan and Tutankhamun was inaugurated as king. He could only ascend the throne by claiming some kind of divinity, and his "excuse" is written on his inauguration inscription. He claimed that his exceptional qualities were evident as soon as he was born, and that the "God" Horus always intended that he should be king (Pinch 2002: 87).

As Pinch points out, many pretending kings claimed that they, like Horus, had been chosen to rule. It was the inauguration "rituals" that turned the chosen heir into a king (2002: 87). This could evidently be done without the right genealogical connection to the remote source of power and the first ancestors. These also seem to have been forgotten up until the New Kingdom. The use of statues to represent individual predecessors is not observed until the New Kingdom. Before, ancestors were worshiped as a collective, and no single ruler was distinguished in the group. They were all called "Followers of Horus." Kings of the distant past (Frankfort 1978 [1948]: 90). Such a time lapse gave ample opportunity for an illegitimate ruler to tamper with the genealogy to fit his purpose, to present himself as truly divine.

Luckily, for the pretending king, the early king lists from the First Dynasty were buried with the kings and were not recovered until 1985. These early lists refute Menes as a historical figure. It seem that Menes is only a fictive figure (or somebody else's ancestor inserted for legitimizing purpose of a pretending "king").

Narmer's existence has been widely documented, and a large number of *serekhs* featuring his name have been excavated during the last twenty-five years in Israel and Palestine, signifying strong commercial links to this area (Raffaele 2003: 109). Egypt had established a series of "colonies" in the south of Palestine aimed at obtaining resources directly. Egyptians also set up a great many seasonal sites in north Sinai from where they imported, for example, wine. Egyptian presence is particularly evident in Tel Erani, 'En Besor, Nahal Tilluh, Tel Malhata, Lachish and Farah from where the Egyptians acquired local products such as copper, asphalt, oil, and wine (Aubet 2013: 214).

In these places, *serekhs* were also fond of Horus Ka, indicating that trade with these places was orchestrated by the ruling elite in Upper Egypt (Aubet 2013: 214–15). Thought-provoking, there are no mentions in these places of any Lower Egyptian figures. Narmer's grave is located in the necropolis

(B) of Abydos and is called tomb B17/18. It consists of two united rectangular mud-brick lined chambers a little north of the grave of his successor Aha (Raffaele 2003: 110). There is no grave for anyone called Menes.

After Narmer, the history of Ancient Egypt becomes sinister. There is no doubt that the rulers became increasingly wealthy and that they therefore gained extraordinary power and status. In the ancient worldview, this could only be explained as a result of direct descent from the remote ancestors, making the "king" divine according to a Western understanding of the world. The way the rulers signaled their status is perhaps more questionable. They chose to take a large number of followers with them into their graves. These burials have been called "retainer-graves," but in fact they look much like human sacrifice. These burials do, however, signal that social stratification had become extreme and that Ancient Egypt had become abundantly wealthy—or at least that some segments of society had.

At this time, Egyptian society was also entering a stage with a more coherent symbolic system, including written records. That is why this period is referred to as the transition from prehistory to history. Symbolic expression had long existed in the form of pictograms designating specific roles or objects, such as instruments for accounting and titles, but from this point onwards the pictograms began to be joined together to form "histories" or events, ultimately developing into proper writing. This advanced symbolism has to be translated, a process which involves juxtaposing two very different worldviews featuring vastly different category systems and conceptualizations of the forces that govern the world.

As a result, many "picture" stories are almost incomprehensible and are mostly left uninterpreted (Tomb 100). Others have given rise to intense debate about how to interpret them, giving free reign to speculation and elaborate explanations (Narmer Palette), while others are "translated" with great confidence, despite mostly being based on long lines of associations (Kings' titles).

This period coincided with the climax of Uruk's colonial expansion into Upper Mesopotamia, and was followed by a massive influx of Mesopotamian objects into Egypt (Aubet 2013: 213). Mesopotamian influence is particularly obvious in the Narmer palette and in the "niched" style used in the construction of monumental mud-brick enclosures at Hierakonpolis, for instance. It is evident in the use of cylinder seals to inscribe containers and in some decorative figures such as the master of beasts and intertwined imaginary feline animals (Wenke 2009: 235). In fact, it seems that the famous Tomb 100, also called "the painted tomb," whose pictures featured many of these symbols as well as a niched structure, could well have been the resting place of a Mesopotamian nobleman. We simply do not know the extent of interaction between these two cultures.

There seems to be one significant reason for the momentous developments in Ancient Egyptian society at this time. The A-group in Nubia suddenly "vanished," and Nubians were thenceforth mostly known as bowmen and mercenaries in the Egyptian army (Midant-Reynes 2000: 224–225). It seems that Egypt annexed the A-group, or rather its territory. This is all archeologically documented.

Because of this annexation, one family came to control all the gold deposits along the Nile valley. The head of this family became known as the Pharaoh. It therefore also seems that the First Dynasty was not a result of the unification of the "Two Lands," Upper and Lower Egypt, but rather of the annexation of Nubia and its gold resources. Lower Egypt played a minor role in Egyptian evolution at this time. Lower Egyptian tradesmen remained what they had always been—intermediaries in trade. No need to aggravate these traders by conquering them. They served their purpose. Moreover, there is no archeological evidence of such an event.

In the light of the importance of the annexation of Nubia, you may be wondering how we should understand the uniting of "The Two Lands" which seems to be reflected in the rulers' titles and headgear ("crowns") from this moment in history onwards. Suffice it to say at this point that the Egyptians themselves have gone to great lengths to explain this situation in different media. You can find their explanation, for example, in the first plate in "The Papyrus of Ani" that forms part of "The Egyptian Book of the Dead." You can also find it in the pictorial rendering on the right hand side of the plate 1-B. Interestingly, the same plate also provides an explanation for the rulers' two types of headgear (Faulkner and Goelet 2015: plate 1-B).

However, the Egyptian rulers had, by now, become the "oil magnates" of the ancient world, dealing instead in gold, and controlling the world's largest deposits at the time. In addition, demand for gold from the East seems to have increased steadily. In Mesopotamia, the so-called Jemdet Nasr period was at its zenith, and seal cylinders poured into Egypt for the first time (Rice 1993: 66), indicating a vast increase in trade. This was also a time when Mesopotamia began to expand its maritime interests in the Persian Gulf, all the while developing a trade network that reached all the way to the mouth of the Indus valley (Wengrow 2006: 142). Egypt seems to have been incorporated increasingly into the Mesopotamian economic orbit.

DYNASTIC ERA

After Narmer, the new wealthy "kings" suddenly started to initiate huge building projects. Large funerary monuments are the most obvious sign of this shift. These new monuments have no real precedent in Egypt (Rice

1993: 116). They introduced a repetitive design of recessed paneling and but-tressing on the facades. This design is borrowed from the facades of temple buildings in Sumer, in particular those belonging to the Jemdet Nasr period. Rice finds that these tombs are very reasonable representations of Sumerian temples, "a circumstance that could hardly be the consequence of chance" (Rice 1993: 119). Suddenly, Egyptian "kings" were buried in Mesopotamian "temples."

Likewise, the emblem that represents the "king," the so-called *serekh*, is made to look as the façade of the tombs. The *serekh* is made as an enclo-sure that resembles a tomb/palace facade in which the name of the "king" is written. The closest contemporary parallel to these crenelated structures has been found on an engraved cylinder seal from Tell Billa in Northern Meso-potamia. These designs appear to be without precedent in Egypt, while the development of the same kind of crenelated architecture can be followed in detail through Mesopotamian history (Mark 2006: 62–63). Contrary to the Egyptians, the Sumerians had a thousand-year long tradition of sophisticated architecture (Rice 2003: 119).

To construct these new structures with the precision that they did, the Egyptians must, at the very least, have had people at their disposal who could supervise them and who had knowledge about the necessary processes involved. This was not just a fleeting change in fashion, or a new invention. These buildings were enormous and all the subsequent "kings" of the First Dynasty built them, suggesting an established policy rather than the random borrowing of an idea from a distant culture (Rice 2003: 119).

These structures also show that Egypt had come into close contact with Mesopotamia, which had become a major trading partner. The only thing that could have instigated this Mesopotamian interest was Egyptian gold, the prestige item par excellence in Mesopotamia. However, we do not know the exact nature of this exchange. It is unlikely that the Egyptians suddenly began to construct Mesopotamian buildings on their own initiative. Did the Egyptians import Mesopotamian artisans? Was the first "king" of Egypt actu-ally of Mesopotamian origin? Or, is there some other explanation? We cannot know. We only know that the ruling stratum in Egypt suddenly started to act very "Mesopotamian."

Anyhow, these new constructions show that Mesopotamian interests had penetrated far into Egyptian territory. Close trading relationships obviously involved cultural dissemination—but only from Mesopotamia to Egypt, not the other way around. In parts of north Mesopotamia, other people also encountered the people from Uruk. In these places, the local elites acted as intermediaries between their own hinterland and the Mesopotamian colonies and they adopted typical Sumerian status elements. It seems that by emu-lating Mesopotamian styles and habits the local "chiefs" increased and legitimized their power (Aubet 2013: 177). The same thing seems to have happened in Egypt.

These new Egyptian kings also began to build large mud-brick enclosures. These were all rectangular, measuring approximately 90x50 m with the largest reaching 130x70 m, and all had rather thick walls, up to 5 m and a height of up to 11 m. These enclosures also had niched facades (Wengrow 2009: 247). Eight of these structures can be dated to the so-called First Dynasty; two to the Second. These structures were also surrounded by "subsidiary burials'": 269 burials around an enclosure that probably belonged to Djer; 80 around one from the time of Den; and 154 from the reign of Djet. About 231 small graves were also discovered in the Western Desert at North Saqqara, which also look like sacrificial burials (Wengrow 2009: 246). These "kings" seem to have been fond of taking lives.

The interior of these enclosures leaves little clue as to their function, and it is uncertain who built which (Wengrow 2009: 244). Nevertheless, at the enclosure at Hierakonpolis, thought to have been built by Kasekhemui, we get a hint as to what it was used for. Its center was occupied by a brick building of unknown purpose, and within the enclosure was a relief composition made of pink granite. On one fragment, the "king" is depicted wearing the "White Crown" and on another a kiosk is depicted, suggesting that the enclosure was used in the *sed*-festival (Wengrow 2009: 248). It seems that these enclosures also shared a kind of ritual similarity to the "kings" burial constructions, having the same outward appearance as well as "subsidiary burials" (Wengrow 2009: 249).

Ancient Egypt's so-called glory era, which started with Narmer, reached even greater heights under his successors. At least the graves got progressively larger. Djer was the second ruler after Narmer. His building at Saqqara measures 56x24 m and the central chamber was originally paneled in wood inlaid with strips of gold plating. Around the building was a low platform upon which was mounted a display of 300 bulls' heads modelled in clay and with actual horns set into place (Rice 1993: 124). A little later, Enezib's grave building contained a hidden buried step pyramid within its superstructure, probably symbolizing the primeval mound that the Egyptians believed had given life to the first humans (gods), a forerunner to Djorser's famous first free-standing step pyramid build in the next dynasty.

This period also offers us a first glimpse into Ancient Egyptian cosmology, that is, the way they conceived of their surrounding world. On an ivory comb belonging to '"King" Djet there are some early hieroglyphs that indicate that he ruled the realms that the sun encircled. His *serekh* is shown with a boat above it sailing the sky with a Horus sitting atop it, borne by large wings (Manley 2013: 118). From later sources, we know that the sun encircles the realm of the living and the so-called afterlife. To get to the meaning of this image, we need to know more about Egyptian cosmology. This is the first glimpse of Egyptian cosmology, which is badly needed if we are to understand Egyptian practices.

Another example from this period that relates to Egyptian cosmology and our understanding of Egyptian kingship comes from an ivory label of "King" Den, the fifth "king" after Narmer. This depiction has come to be emblematic of Egyptian kinship throughout the ages. Perhaps for the first time, we have an image that contains something that resembles hieroglyphs and which would seem to hold greater promise in terms of understanding the message conveyed.

In the picture, we see Den identified by a *serekh*. He stands with his right arm raised holding a mace-like instrument, towering above a man in a kind of kneeling position, one leg in front of the other. This is interpreted as representing the king who is about to strike an enemy, and the following "text" on the label is read accordingly. Although the proto-hieroglyphs are hard to read, the text on the left side of Den is translated as, "it is the bull" meaning the "king." The text on the right side is translated as the "first occasion for slaughtering the east(erners)," and the "text" in the middle is even more obscure but seems to give the easterners' numbers or place of origin (Manley 2013: 120).

To a large extent, this standard interpretation of the scene is predetermined by an understanding of the Egyptian rulers as conquerors. This motif is known as "smiting the enemy," who most often comes from "the east." To be sure, even experts find the message cryptic (Manley 2013: 121). This is further complicated by the way the figures are represented in the picture, which really does not look at all like an execution. It is much too complicated: in his left hand, Den is holding a long stick and some kind of softer material that bends over the head of the kneeling man, and perplexingly they are both holding onto these in the same place and seemingly pressing them towards the kneeling man's head. With the other hand, the kneeling man is holding onto Den's lower leg.

Rather than an execution or battle scene, it seems that the figures are united in some form of "ritual." In addition, the reference to the king as "bull" stems from a translation of the hieroglyph "upraised hands" on the left hand side of Den as "bull"—even though the sign denoting "upraised hands" is most often translated as *ka*. *Ka* is usually translated as "a person's double," but without knowledge about Egyptian personhood we cannot say for sure what this entity is or does. Still, it would give a completely new twist to the interpretation of the scene in question. Seen from this alternative perspective, it would mean "it is his '*ka*'" that is doing something.

By the time of Den, there is ample evidence of sustained and intensive contact between Egypt and the Near East (Wilkinson 2006: 77). Additionally, the "king" felt obliged to add a new title to his titular: namely '*swt-bíty*, rendered as a sedge plant and a bee, which Egyptologists translate literally as "he of the reed and bee" (Wilkinson 2006: 75) (strangely this "title" is later attribute to Menes who would have been contemporaneously with Narmer—before the title was introduced). However, the bee is also identified with the "god" Min (Rice 1991: 124). Den also invented a "double crown" that combined the older red and white "crowns."

Still, material culture progressed. So did the political organization of the land. However, these seem to have been sinister times. Apart from the many subsidiary burials, there is also some evidence that other forms of human sacrifice were practiced. On an ivory label from Djer's reign, two men are depicted facing each other. One appears to be plunging a knife into the other person's breast, holding a vessel underneath to catch the victim's blood (Rice 1993: 121).

Times were changing and so, apparently, was the role of the "kings." Qaa is listed as the first dynasty's last king on the various king lists. After his reign, something seems to have gone wrong. Aside from the fact that some became unhealthily rich while others lives were sacrificed in this period, a thousand years of nearly continuous progress ended. The period that followed is called the Second Dynasty (c. 2890–c. 2670 BCE), the first of several downturns in Egyptian history.

On the positive side, subsidiary burials ended. During the First Dynasty, we know of at least 1066 such burials. In addition, the character of the rulers' names changed (see also Manley 2013: 136). In the first dynasty, all the "kings" have predatory-sounding names, for example, Narmer translates as catfish or "Striker," Aha is "Horus the Fighter," Djet is "Horus or cobra who Strikes," and Den is "Horus who Strikes." Djer is the exception that confirms the rule, being known as "Horus who Succors."

In the second dynasty, the first king is called Hotepsekhemwy (Hetepsekhemwy), which translates as "Pleasing in Powers." His name has also been interpreted to mean "two powerful ones are at peace." The second ruler was called Raneb (or Nebra), which translates as "Re is the Lord," and the last king of the dynasty was called Khasekhemwy, which translates as "The Two Powerful Ones Appear."

Between the two dynasties, there seems to have been quite a change in approach to the rulers' names: from evoking a conquering force, the names came to denote a mediating role between opposites; instead of aggressors, they evoked "religious" or cosmological themes (Manley 2013: 136). Peribsen, who ruled just before Khasekhemwy, exemplifies this cosmological understanding of a ruler. He was known for encouraging literacy and religious thought.

Indeed, the first complete sentence that we know of comes from his reign. It reads,

> The golden one, he of Ombos, hath unified and handed over the two realms to his son, the king of Lower and Upper Egypt, Peribsen. (Mark, J. J. 2016)

This also suggests that the cosmological aspect of rule was enhanced during the second dynasty. We just have to get to grips with the meaning of "handed over the two *realms* to his son" (note: realms not lands).

In addition to this, at the start of the Second Dynasty a thoroughgoing destruction took place of the graves from the first dynasty. All the tombs of the previous kings from the First Dynasty and their officials were destroyed in immense fires across the whole country (Rice 1993: 129). In addition, the more modest graves in Helwan also seem to have been destroyed by fire. According to Rice, these fires indicate hostility by the Egyptians of the Second Dynasty towards their First Dynasty predecessors (Rice 1993: 133).

There seems to have been something of a rebellion against the "Strikers" and "Fighters" of the First Dynasty, and a replacement of them with more benevolent rulers who appeased the powers that the Egyptians believed to rule the cosmos. Splendor seems to have diminished in importance, and not much is known about the rulers of the Second Dynasty.

Romer simply calls this "The Lost Dynasty" (2013: 215), mostly because we do not know much about it. This may be due to scarce archeological data, but it could also reflect real world changes. Alas, meanwhile, in another part of the world—one highly interconnected to Egypt and the rulers of the First Dynasty—the so-called Uruk expansion in Mesopotamia ground to a halt. Mesopotamia experienced a period of ruralization and decentralization (Akkermans and Schwartz 2003: 224). In some areas, contact was broken off with Mesopotamia forever. This period is also known as the Uruk collapse (Akkermans and Schwartz 2003: 207).

Relations between Egypt and the north of Sinai and Palestine were broken off, and the Egyptian colonies were abandoned (Aubet 2013: 217). The Egyptian recession was not a localized phenomenon. Egyptian imports and exports suffered in these dire times, and this would have had social consequences within Egypt. This situation could explain both the anger against the previous rulers, who may have been seen as having corrupted the system with their extravagance; and at the lesser role played by the rulers of most of the Second Dynasty. If the market shrinks and the all-important prestige goods become rarer, the locals search for explanations, and in ancient times and in kinship-based societies, blame could only have been targeted against the ancestors (as we know from anthropology), as they would have been seen as responsible for orchestrating contemporary conditions. This seems like a plausible reason for blaming the previous rulers.

At the end of this period, called the Ninevite 5 (ca. 3100–2550 BC), large territorial transformations took place, with a significant growth of the main urban centers in the Near East, such as Tell Brak, Halawa, and Tell al-Raqa'i. It seems that Egyptian exchange relations with the Levant were reorganized and that instead of overland trade routes, a sea route was established to Byblos situated on the present day Lebanese coast twenty-five miles north of Beirut.

Byblos developed into an important commercial center in the Eastern Mediterranean world (Jidejian 1972: 1). It was to become the major trading port for Egypt for a long time to come. Maritime trade considerably reduces distances and bigger ships allowed for more cargo and thereby reduced the cost of timber, wine, and oil (Aubet 2013: 219).

Up until this point, the rulers of the Second Dynasty were rather inconspicuous: not much is known about them, and they have left very few traces. Nevertheless, by Khasekhemwy's time this had all changed. He was known in Byblos. In the Egyptian temple area here, a fragment of a stone vessel was found that is inscribed with the phrase "Khasekhemwy, given life" (Wilkinson 1999: 92). Egyptian foreign relations were apparently back on track and attained new heights under Khasekhemwy, as evidenced by the fact that he appointed an "overseer of foreign lands." Back in business, he also built a truly impressive "mortuary" construction at Abydos that measured 70x17 m at one end, and 10 m at the other. It featured a burial chamber lined with blocks of dressed limestone (Wilkinson 1999: 92).

Khasekhemwy also built several monumental enclosures at Abydos and Hierakonpolis. Especially the enclosure at Abydos is impressive. It measures 123x64 m, with walls as thick as 5 m and as high as 20 m. The inner walls were niched, and inside the enclosure there was a roughly square mound of sand and gravel covered with mud brick. This is located in a similar position in the enclosure as Djoser's later Step Pyramid (Tour Egypt 2016a). Khasekhemwy buried a fleet of boats adjacent to the enclosure at Abydos, and there is evidence of other major building projects from his reign (Wilkinson 1999: 93). He was "by far the most prolific builder of the Early Dynastic period as a whole" (Wilkinson 1999: 93).

His tomb treasures also attest to his wealth. Among these are a scepter made of a type of stone known as *sard* that has bands of gold, limestone vases with sheet gold covers, and a bronze basin (Wilkinson 1999: 93–94). This is the first appearance of bronze in Egypt (Wenke 2009: 246). From the Palermo stone, we also know that Khasekhemwy fashioned a copper statue of himself called 'high is Khasekhemwy' (Wilkinson 1999: 94). On this statue, Khasekhemwy is wearing the close-fitting robe associated with the so-called *sed* festival (Wilkinson 1999: 94). Khasekhemwy died in about 2686 BC (Tour Egypt 2016b).

Following the Uruk collapse, things were also beginning to speed up in Mesopotamia. We are now entering what has been called the Early Dynastic III Period (beginning *circa* 2600 BC). Small farming villages had, by now, become consolidated as thriving centers of industry. Southern Mesopotamia was divided into twenty to thirty independent city states, each with its own dependent smaller towns and villages (Zettler and Horne 1998: 4). In Syria, the period is known as the "Second Urban Revolution," in which Syria experienced one of the most important transformations in its history. We are witnessing a fully fledged adaptation of urban life (Akkermans and Schwartz 2009: 211). Life was suddenly changing in the Middle East, and the Egyptian market for gold expanded immensely.

Ur was one of the southern Mesopotamian city states, and the best known, thanks to Sir Leonard Wooley. In 1927–1928, he excavated sixteen royal graves in the cemetery at Ur belonging to the so-called Early Dynastic III period. These graves were exceptionally splendid and eerie. They contained great wealth and large numbers of human sacrifices (Woolley 1928 [1965]: 59). All sixteen graves contained large amounts of gold jewelry. The grave of a "king" called Mes-kalam-dug contained, among other fine objects, gold daggers, hundreds of gold beads, heavy gold bowls, a gold head-dress, and most famous of all, a gold helmet fashioned as a wig (Woolley 1963: 58). "As an example of goldsmith's work this is the most beautiful thing we have found in the cemetery" (Woolley 1963: 59).

If the graves at Ur are in any way representative of royal splendor in the twenty to thirty Mesopotamian city states—not to mention all the royal courts in what is now Syria—there must have been great quantities of gold in circulation. For a long time to come, Egypt had a steady and growing market for its gold. Egypt was the place to go to obtain gold. This is clearly indicated in a letter written to the later Pharaoh Akhenaten by an Assyrian king. Having just received a gift from the Pharaoh that he thought unworthy, he wrote,

> Is it from a great king, a gift such as this? Gold is dust in your land—one simply gathers it up . . . I intend to build a new palace. Send me enough gold for its decoration and its furnishing. . . . If in good faith your intention is friendship then send me much gold. (Kriwaczek 2012: 222)

At this time, Byblos was Egypt's major trading post. From Khasekhemwy's reign onwards, this relationship with Byblos only deepened. No other site has yielded such quantities of Egyptian imports as Byblos, and almost all the Pharaohs of the so-called Old Kingdom sent presents to Byblos inscribed with their names (Aubet 2013: 231). These gifts were probably intended to strengthen the trade that Byblos mediated via its large hinterland that reached all the way to Southern Mesopotamia.

At long last, we are entering the period that most people associate with Ancient Egypt: the age of the pyramids. This new trade route to Byblos and its vastly increased capacity obviously made the Egyptians—or at least the Pharaohs—tremendously rich. They could afford anything they wanted. Anthropology tells us that, according to their worldview, they would have had to be well connected to their remote ancestors to be able to accomplish this. From the outside, and certainly from the point of view of a different category system, the Pharaohs appeared as divine, and they acted as such. To attract such wealth, they would have had to be the direct descendants of the primordial beings.

With riches flowing in, the Egyptian elite also changed the organization of its tribute system, formalizing it. This change is clearly reflected in two graves, one from the First Dynasty and one from the Third. From the first dynasty, we have the grave of a man called Merka. He seems to have been employed in taking care of the supplies and conduct of the royal court. He died during the reign of Qa'a, the last ruler of the first dynasty (Romer 2013: 251–252).

Merka had an enormous and elaborate grave. Like all First Dynasty graves, it had been consumed by fire and ransacked (Romer 2013: 252). From a granite stelae that was found in one of the corridors, we know that Merka had many titles, and that he was probably a central figure at the royal court, partaking in the annual round of voyaging and court appearances to collect tribute around the country. Merka belonged to a cast of specialists who had the skills to organize the court and its regalia, and to count and circulate the goods it accumulated on these yearly trips around the country (Romer 2013: 255). Marka's grave gives us insight into how the tribute system worked at the end of the first dynasty: namely that the 'king' went on annual trips to collect his tribute. He probably also gave some form of prestige goods (wine, oil, etc.) in return, at least to the local noble men who could then distribute it among their people.

Just a few hundred meters from Merka's grave, another enormous grave was uncovered belonging to a man called Hesi-re. This man and his grave belonged to the reign of Djoser of the Third Dynasty (Romer 2013: 258). In this grave, some remarkable drawings were found of furniture, beds, stools, sticks, cabinets, canopies mats, you name it. In another section, the walls were decorated with images of weights and measures of oil jars, boxes of tools, utensils and supplies. The real objects that had been deposited in First dynasty graves were replaced in this third dynasty grave by mere painted images of objects (Romer 2013: 262–63). Images and written words had taken on a special power: real provisions in former graves had been replaced by symbols in the tomb of Hesi-re.

This shift from real objects to their symbolic renderings seems to be part of a larger restructuring of the Egyptian economy. In First Dynasty graves, one finds a vast number of seal impressions recording the names of officials, like Merka, who were engaged in the traffic and supply of goods. By the Third Dynasty, it was almost exclusively the name of the king that appeared on these seals, and the annual round of tribute collection also seems to have stopped (Romer 2013: 266). Tribute collection seems to have been conducted from regional bases. It seems that the process of tribute collection had become both centralized and formalized, and in the process, the king had elevated himself above such worldly affairs. The Egyptian economy was flourishing. The Pharaohs became tremendously rich. They appeared otherworldly, as though they lived a separate existence.

PYRAMID ERA

Gone are the days of retainer burials: this is the era of monumental buildings. Sacrifices have given way to constructions. And the people toiled on. Enter Djoser. He certainly held himself in high esteem. He also seems to have been tremendously rich, so much so that he was able to alter the practices of former rulers. Indeed, he initiated a completely new practice in Egyptian history: he was intent on building the world's largest stone structure so far.

Like many of his predecessors, Djoser also set out to build an enclosure. It consisted of a limestone wall that was 10, 5 m high and 1,645 m long (Lehner 1997: 84). All previous enclosures had housed some kind of internal construction that has long since disappeared because they were mostly built using flimsy materials. Therefore, it is also difficult to determine what they were used for and what went on inside them. Djoser seemed intent on making his enclosure permanent. He built the entire interior in stone. Thanks to this and to inscriptions in the interior of the "grave" we now know that enclosures were used for, among other things, the *sed* festival.

All the *sed* attributes from later constructions seem to be present in Djoser's enclosure (and therefore in previous enclosures): the court demarcating "territories," and a special dais furnished with "two thrones" for the appearance of the king in different incarnations—often assumed to be representations of Upper and Lower Egypt. To accommodate this interpretation it is also claimed that the depiction of the thrones as standing back to back must be an artistic measure for rendering "a pair which were actually side by side" (Kemp 1995: 59). This is mere speculation. Maybe the Egyptians just meant the depiction to be taken at face value.

Meanwhile, Djoser had more inventions in store. In the spot where Khasekhemwy had built a square mound of sand and gravel covered with mudbrick in his enclosure, Djoser chose to build his *mastaba*. In this way, he combined the "great enclosures" of the former rulers with their burial monuments (Wilkinson 2010: 68). This is probably not a coincidence. It must have had great symbolic significance. In doing so, he claimed a major ritualistic space for himself. This must have completely transformed the way the pharaoh was conceptualized.

Djoser was not finished. Claiming "ritual" space for himself in the enclosure was not enough. He was not content with just placing his *mastaba* at the center of the enclosure. Obviously, he had chosen a ritual space in the enclosure for his *mastaba*, but it seems that having done so he found that it did not quite serve its purpose. Maybe it did not live up to the ritual function of the mound that he was trying to substitute.

It is widely accepted that the step pyramid reflects its origin in *mastab* tombs, and that Djoser simply built six successively smaller *mastabas* one on top of the other (e.g., Wenke 2009: 276). It seems that he was combining the mounds from the enclosures with his own *mastaba*. But a *mastaba* is not a mound, so it had to be made into one. In any case, he decided to extend his *mastaba* in all directions, especially upwards. When finished, its six steps reached a height of 60 m (Lehner 1997: 84). This new form was apparently so essential that the practice continued for centuries.

As with previous *mastabas*, Djoser also needed an underground construction, which would have to be on an unprecedented scale. It consisted of 5.7 km of shafts, tunnels, chambers, galleries and magazines. A central corridor and two parallel ones extend for 365 m, connecting 400 rooms (Lehner 1997: 87). These underground structures were extremely complicated, and even the so-called burial chamber was constructed in a very inconvenient fashion. A central shaft was constructed above a vault, called the burial vault. The shaft was 7 m square and 28 m deep, but the vault seems to have been relocated, the final vault being made of granite, while the first one had walls of alabaster and a pavement of diorite or schist. It also had a limestone roof decorated with large, five-pointed stars in low relief (Lehner 1997: 87).

In another area of this underground world were rows of blue faience tiles and limestones, and three of these were topped by an arch supported by simulated *djed* pillars (Lehner 1997: 88) (associated with Osiris who "ruled" the so-called Netherworld). In some of these underground galleries, remarkable collections of vessels, stacks of plates, and cups mostly made of alabaster and other fine stones were found, amounting to a grand total of around 40,000 vessels. These were not all made for Djoser but many seem to have been taken from First Dynasty graves at Saqqara. Even though these graves had been burned and ransacked, Djoser still seems to have wanted to integrate these rulers' burial possessions into his underground "Kingdom." Ancestors are important, no matter their reputation.

Most surprisingly, the burial vault consisted of solid granite blocks and the only entrance to it was an aperture toward the north that was blocked by a plug weighing 3.5 tons. The aperture is very small, and the space inside the vault is also tiny (Lehner 1997: 87). "Nothing wider than 1 m could be inserted into the chamber," writes Lehner (1997: 88). Not much room for a coffin. Either "King" Djoser must have been a very small man, or something else was at stake here. Nevertheless, he had created an amazing underground world with a mountain of rocks above, neatly stacked into "steps."

Meanwhile, Egypt's economy and social organization were becoming increasingly complicated, and the "royal" family did not have the work force to take care of all the different dimensions of rule. To accommodate these economic challenges, a "vizier" was appointed who reported directly to the "king," as a kind of chief minister, and a host of other offices were also created. Positions were no longer dependent on birthright and on being part of the royal family. Ordinary men could now create their own careers. We know this from a man called Metjen and his tomb inscription. This holds one of the earliest autobiographical texts, describing how he started out as storehouse clerk, moving on to a position in local government, and then being promoted to governor of several Delta provinces, ending up as a trusted courtier (Wilkinson 2010: 69).

Bureaucracy expanded. This was to some extent the result of building pyramids, which required a large logistical apparatus to coordinate the vast amount of resources used to build them. Pyramid building became the fashion for the next thousand years. This situation greatly enhanced the capabilities of the administrative apparatus of Egyptian society.

We know precious little about Djoser's Third Dynasty successors, Sekhemkhet, Khaba, and Sanakht (Wilkinson 2010: 70). Sekhemkhet started an enclosure with an associated pyramid at the center, but died after only a few years in office. His building project stopped and the pyramid only reached its first step, but the subterranean "house" and its "burial" chamber were very advanced. Here, the excavator found a sealed alabaster sarcophagus. It was opened in 1954 under intense media observation, only to be found empty (Romer 2013: 317).

Khaba also started to build a pyramid but this was never finished. Its substructure was similar to Sekhemkhet's but no traces of a burial were found and all the galleries were clean and empty (Lehner 1997: 95). The burial place for the next king remains unknown (Romer 2013: 318). Then something changed. Huni, who was the next king in this dynasty, built not one but seven small pyramids scattered around the country. Each one had three or four steps, and none of them showed any signs or trace of burial arrangements. As Lehner writes, "The purpose of these small step pyramids is a mystery" (1997: 96). Neither has Huni's tomb ever been found (Romer 2013: 318).

As Lehner observes, these small step pyramids "may mark locations of political centres" (1997: 96). If this is the case, all similar structures must be seen as political structures, which at that time and in that place could only mean that they had cosmological significance. Romer suggests that these small pyramids form part of certain rites of audience and offerings that surrounded the king, and that they played the same role as the more centralized ones (Romer 2013: 327).

Therefore, there does not seem to be any strict correspondence between pyramids and actual burials. Pyramids may have served another purpose than merely being burial places for megalomaniac pharaohs. Details of their construction, or any information concerning their use, have never found their way into the annals or been depicted on graves or in any other media (Romer 2013: 355).

So far, there are only two extant references to pyramid building. In 1993, it was decided to clear Sahur's "causeway" and partly restore his "mortuary" temple. During the excavation, workers found twenty limestone blocks carved with reliefs. Nothing remotely like them has ever been found elsewhere. One scene spreading over several blocks gives some insight into pyramid building. It shows a gang of men hauling the pyramidion (the apex of the pyramid made of one piece of stone), with an accompanying inscription which reads "bringing the pyramidion covered with fine gold to the pyramid." Other blocks show the sledge bearing the pyramidion being dragged to the pyramid, while one man is pouring water on the ground in front to reduce friction (Silverman 1997: 189).

In 2013, another find relating to pyramid building was discovered. At the Egyptian shore of the Red Sea at Wadi al-Jarf, a team from the University of Paris-Sorbonne and the IFAO discovered a harbor complex. This site was occupied at the beginning of the 4th dynasty and it was probably used both by Sneferu and Khufu as a harbor for royal expeditions to the copper and turquoise mines located on the opposite site of the Gulf of Suez. It seems to have been closed down soon after the completion of The Great Pyramid.

Here the excavation team discovered several dozen fragments of the oldest inscribed papyri found so far. For some reason, these papyri were left here. They belonged to a man called Merer. He was a gang-leader of a team of some 200 men working at the construction of The Great Pyramid. As it turned out, the papyri were his log-book, recording the team's work schedule at the pyramid.

Merer was in charge of transporting the limestone casing from Tura to the construction site. These casing stones were brought to the pyramid site by boat along the River Nile and a system of canals. One boat trip between Tura and the pyramid site, a distance of about 10 km, took four days to complete, the logbook notes (Pierre and Gregory 2014: 4–14).

We do, therefore, know something about the construction of pyramids. But we do not know anything about the actual funerals, nor do any accounts exist of these. Everyday practices seem to have been amply recorded inside graves, but strangely there are no depictions of large funeral possessions entering a pyramid, of the whereabouts of the dead "king," or of the coronation of new "kings." To be sure, there were plenty of opportunities for recording such events. At least thirty-five of these structures were built (Lehner 1997: 17).

It is possible that these celebrations were either so "ordinary" or formalized that they did not need to be described to a contemporary audience or for posterity. Still, many other highly formalized occasions like the *sed*-festival found their way into pictorial and written testimonies. Alternatively, such festive funeral practices may have been described in ways that are not immediately clear to present day audiences.

Still, building pyramids seems by now to have become an obsession. Sneferu was the next king in line, and the first of the fourth dynasty. For some reason, he felt compelled to construct three pyramids, for which he quarried, transported and set up some twenty million tons of cut stone blocks (Romer 2013: 320). First, he built a step pyramid at Meidum that, quite tellingly, is called *Djet Sneferu*, a title that Lehner translates as "Sneferu Endures" (1997: 97). *Djet* pillars are often associated with "the resurrection of Osiris," king of the so-called Netherworld especially in the form *Banebdjedet* (the *ba* of the lord (*neb*) of the *Djedet*) (Crystalinks 216).

He initially left this pyramid unfinished. He had other plans. He went on to build two pyramids at Dahshur. Here, he built the so-called Bent Pyramid and the North, or Red, Pyramid. According to conventional wisdom, the Bent Pyramid is a mistake. It is thought that it was initially meant to be taller with a raising angle of 72 degrees but due to structural problems, the slope had to be reduced midway to 43 degrees giving the pyramid a characteristic "bend" (Lehner 1997: 102).

At the same time, Sneferu started on his third pyramid. This was built from the start using the same slope as the top part of the Bent Pyramid. After this he went back to the Meidum pyramid and finished this as a "true" pyramid. He obviously needed two almost aligned pyramids, or else he would have used the building blocks from the 'malformed' and damaged pyramid for his ultimate burial place. In all probability, they were built according to plan, despite the much-acclaimed problems with the Bent Pyramid. He wanted the Bent Pyramid finished, despite its so-called flaws. This situation with two aligned pyramids (and one in reserve) cast further doubt on pyramids being intended only as funeral places.

Sneferu also made some major stylistic changes to the pyramid. From now on, pyramids would have pointed apexes (a capstone) and smooth surfaces. The capstone was called a pyramidion. It was made of one block of granite or limestone covered with gold or electrum (Silverman 1997: 171). These new pyramids would have been splendidly white as they were covered with white limestone. Features that would not have been possible with the step pyramid. This is a major cultural change in royal symbolism.

Sneferu also changed the substructure. Gone are the long underground corridors and the many magazines and galleries. In the case of the Meidum pyramid, we see instead a more simple construction with a long corridor starting 16.6 m up the facade leading *downwards* to a vertical shaft that is connected to an inside chamber (called the burial chamber). This chamber has the first recorded corbelling ceiling, looking much like a *djet* pillar (sign for the "Netherworld"). It was very small, 5.9 m x 2.65 m and never finished (Lehner 1997: 98).

It seems that the *mastabas* concept no longer served its purpose, not even when they were stacked on top of each other. One cannot, therefore, speak of any natural evolution towards a "true" pyramid. The two types served different purposes. We may infer this new purpose from Sneferu's titles. As his so-called Horus name, Sneferu took the phrase *neb Maat*, which commonly translates as "lord of truth." But *Maat* was also the reason for the existence of the universe. *Maat* transformed the primeval chaos into the present order. *Neb* did not just mean "lord" but also "owner" and "keeper" (Wilkinson 2010: 73). Sneferu, then, was more or less the "owner of existence." To underline this point, Sneferu also adopted a new title, *netjer nefer* (Wilkinson 2010: 73), or "the perfect god."

Quirke writes that *netjer nefer* can also translate as "younger god" on earth, standing in contrast to *netjer 'aa* which means "elder god" in heaven (2015: 96). Except that, such a division between earth and heaven seems more European than Egyptian. In Egypt, the sun *Re* sailed on the primeval water above in "heaven" during the day and beneath in the "Netherworld" at night. Maybe Sneferu was trying to connect these two realms of existence by building both upwards towards the sky and downward to create a chamber underground.

Sneferu called the pyramid at Dahshur "Appearance" (Wilkinson 2010: 76), the same expression that is used for the human body in life (Lehner 1997: 22). It might seem an obvious name given that the pyramid is majestically huge and awe-inspiring, but it begs the question: "appearance" of what? It must have meant something because this structure became the prototype for every subsequent pyramid.

This building frenzy required both a vast administrative system and a massive amount of resources. From the Palermo Stone, we know that in the fourteenth year of Sneferu's reign he started thirty-five royal estates with accompanying workforces, and 122 cattle farms. Most of the yield from these estates went straight to the royal palace. Ordinary people must have made a much more meager living, since the cereals grown on the estates were preferentially fed to the cattle, rather than to the human subjects that took care of these animals (Wilkinson 2010: 77). "The perfect god" was not a benign god.

Sneferu had close relations with Byblos. From the Palermo Stone we know that he brought forty ships from Byblos, loaded with cedar and pine wood destined to build forty-four boats, the gate of the royal palace and the roof of his "burial chambers" (Aubet 2013: 232). Later, Sneferu ordered a ship some fifty-two meters long to be built (Aubert 2013: 232). Sneferu obviously had the means to raise resources.

From Sneferu's reign onwards, Byblos had regular and intense relations with the pharaohs (Aubet 2013: 232). It appears that Byblos was, by now, the main destination for the commercial interests of the Egyptian royal court, and almost all the pharaohs from this time onwards had relations with Byblos, as testified to by their gifts and offerings to the city (Aubet 2013: 232).

Sneferu's son, Khufu (also known as Cheops in Greek), took the art of pyramid building to a completely new level. He built one of the seven wonders of the ancient world, and the only one still standing: "The Great Pyramid of Khufu." No building had ever been so elaborate and exact, and nothing would match it in the future. There seems to have been no limit to the work and resources that were used to build this construction. Its sheer mass, precision in construction, and its elaborate internal system of galleries, rooms and corridors are breath-taking—astonishing and unparalleled. It seems to hail from another world (and indeed some think that it does). He only needed one pyramid but he gave it a double name: *The pyramid that is the place of sunrise and sunset* (Vendel, 2016a). Maybe we should not just see this as a poetic expression (as suggested), but as an accurate description of its purpose, strange as this might seem in the contemporary Western world (a good guess here would be that Sneferu had separate pyramids for sunrise and sunset, respectively).

Curiously, the "entrance" was again located high up on the façade, with a *descending* corridor leading underground to a roughly cut chamber some 30 m below ground. From the corridor there is an ascending corridor leading to a point where it splits into a corridor running horizontally to a small chamber (called the "Queens chamber"), and one leading to a "grand gallery" that connects to the "burial chamber" (called the "Kings chamber").

"Air shafts" run from the two chambers toward the exterior. These either stop at "false doors" or do not lead all the way into the rooms. Therefore, these shafts do not let in any air, and indeed one might ask why air could possibly have been needed in the chambers (this feature is only found in this pyramid). Located above the "King's chamber" are "relieving chambers" made of long granite blocks (Lehner 1997: 108) (this "chamber" also looks very much like the *djet* pillars found in all other pyramids).

Khufu seems to have needed three rooms for his "burial." Well, if the room with the sarcophagus was for his body, and the "Queens chamber" was for his *ka*-statue, then the underground chamber has no apparent purpose. The Old Greek historian, Herodotus (born about 490 BCE), sparked some speculation about the burial of Khufu. Having interviewed some priests some 2000 years later (which is by all means a very long time even in Egypt), he reports that

> the underground chambers which Cheops (Khufu) intended as vaults for his own use: these last were built on a sort of island surrounded by water introduced from the Nile by a canal. (Rice 1993: 205)

According to Rice, scholars have universally discounted this idea. There is no evidence whatsoever of a subterranean lake (Rice 1993: 205). This still leaves the underground room unexplained.

Many have marveled over this pyramid. In AD 1798 Napoleon camped his soldiers at the foot of the plateau, telling his men, "Soldiers of France, forty centuries gaze down upon you" (Wilkinson 2010: 87). It seem only fair to ask, with Wilkinson, what the purpose of this grandiose project was, and why ten thousand people would toil for more than twenty years to build an artificial mountain of stone? (Wilkinson 2010: 86). Egyptologists largely believe that building pyramids is the ultimate expression of divine kingship. For Wilkinson, it was the projection of ultimate power. Something despots do in a kind of *folies de grandeur* (Wilkinson 2010: 87).

However, there are some rather strange features in these constructions, which suggest that this is not the whole story. The passage leading to the "burial chamber" is only about 1.05 m wide and a little taller before opening up to the "Grand Gallery" (Lehner 1997: 111). It must have been a painstaking job to bring Khufu to his final resting place. It is as if these constructions were never meant to accommodate funerals.

Their special designs must have meant something more to the Ancient Egyptians. Pyramids must represent something in the Egyptian cosmology—some principle that they considered important enough to make structures in this particular form. The purpose of the pyramids is far from self-evident. Pyramids are also too special to be random reflections of megalomaniac pharaohs. There is too much repetition. The consistency of the pyramidal form does not bear the mark of individual ambitions but of cultural necessity. Pharaohs could not *not* build a pyramid. For some reason.

Khufu also had contact with Byblos as did all the other pharaohs of the 4th dynasty. In Byblos, an alabaster vase was found inscribed with Khufu's name. He also imported a cedar wood boat. It was discovered in 1954, dismantled and deposited in a sealed pit, cut into the rock at the foot of the Great

Pyramid. When reconstructed, it was 43.32 m long and weighed a total of 150 tons, with a loading capacity of 50 tons (Aubet 2013: 232–3). Quite a ship.

In 1925, the archeologist Reisner's photographer was setting up his tripod close to the Great Pyramid. One leg sank into the ground. It turned out he had placed it on a sealed shaft. This shaft turned out to be 27 m deep. It was blocked with masonry. It took the archeological team weeks to clear. At the bottom, they found a little room (Lehner 1997: 117). Two months later, they were able to establish that it belonged to the wife of Sneferu and the mother of Khufu. Her name was Hetepheres (Romer 2013: 391). It was a reburial. It was intact. It took twenty years to restore the content of the room to its original condition (Romer 2013: 392).

The grave contained great treasures, among them an alabaster sarcophagus and a small alabaster box with a string around it, and the sealing on both was intact. So, once again, there was an intact, sealed sarcophagus. And once again, it was opened with great anticipation. Once again, when the lid slid open, it was "as empty as the day it had been made" (Romer 2013: 392). They had more "luck" with the smaller box. It contained four small packets of her entrails.

There have been many attempts to account for the missing body in this and other sealed sarcophaguses. Among them, we have the usual suspects—grave robbers. For Hetephere's burial, the story goes something like this: the original grave was robbed, the body stolen, and therefore it was necessary to carry out a secret reburial (Lehner 1997: 117). Why the "grave robbers" wanted the body, and not the treasures, is left unexplained. Or maybe the officials in charge of the new (secret) grave had to refurnish it.

At any rate, a pattern seems to be emerging of empty sarcophaguses and pyramids with no traces of funerals. Maybe we should take the missing bodies seriously, instead of trying to ignore them. Maybe the "burial places" were intended to be "empty" (seen in a Western perspective). If so, there has to be a cultural explanation for this.

Apart from all the treasures, the entrails are perhaps the most significant find in Hetepheres's tomb. That these were taken out of the body and stored separately is often explained as a solution to the difficulties that these organs pose to the mummification process. This is a very practical and functional explanation. Still, the Ancient Egyptians left the heart in the body. This would pose the same problem as the entrails but it was not solved in the same way. Something else seems to be going on. Instead of a practical explanation, we need a symbolic/cultural explanation for this custom.

The devil is in the detail. The separately buried entrails carry a potent cultural message about the Egyptian understanding of personhood. For anthropologists, separately stored entrails are not a practical solution to decomposing bodies. Instead, the entrails point to a significant cultural conception of the human body, personhood and the way humans relate to the larger world. In many cultures, entrails are seen as an "inside skin" in contrast to the "outside skin" that is the human appearance. Therefore, these finds reflect two different aspects of Ancient Egyptian personhood.

This is a period of intense pyramid building. After a small venture by Djedefre to Abu Roash, Khufu's sons, Khafre and Menkaure, returned to Giza and build their pyramids here. Altogether, Giza has nine pyramids, three big ones and six smaller ones.

In 1818, Khafre's sarcophagus was found by Belzoni. To his disappointment, he found that he was not the first to enter it. Some time in prehistory, someone had deposited bones in the sarcophagus that turned out to be those of a bull, an animal that from later days is known to represent Osiris (Lehner 1997: 124). It could have been an offering. It could be a coincidence that it was a bull. Alternatively, it could have been (representative of) Osiris. In which case, the pyramid could be interpreted as the resting place of Osiris.

A less well-known pharaoh started to build a pyramid that, when finished, would have been the same size as the big pyramids at Giza. His name is uncertain: he is referred to as Nebka, Wehemka and Baka, among others. His pyramid was left unfinished (Lehner 1997: 139). It was excavated at the beginning of the 1900s by an Italian archeologist named Barsanti. He found a rounded sarcophagus sunk into the floor that was paved with huge stones located at the bottom of a big shaft. The lid was intact and sealed with gypsum (Vendel 2016b).

You guessed it. Once again, it was empty. Once again, we have an unfinished pyramid with a sealed sarcophagus. Empty sarcophaguses can no longer been seen as mere coincidences. There seems to be a pattern here. Instead of simple corpse robberies or mere flukes, empty sarcophaguses seem to have been the rule, not the exception. Why steal the body in an unfinished pyramid, and then go to great lengths to seal it?

Ancient Egyptians installed and sealed the sarcophaguses long before the construction of the pyramids was finished, and in certain cases we know that they sealed the sarcophagus *before* the pharaoh died, and when he did, they did not reopen it and bury the Pharaoh in it—instead they gave up the project of finishing the pyramid in question. It seems that the work crews sealed the sarcophaguses as part of the construction of the pyramids, before the pharaohs died. Moreover, since the sarcophaguses were empty, the whereabouts of the corpses of the dead pharaohs are unknown. This leaves us with a case of missing corpses. It is a conundrum.

Nebka's successor was Mankaure. In his pyramid, we find the first decorative elements since Djoser. These consist of a series of panels carved with repeated tall and stylized "false door" motifs (Lehner 1997: 135). All pyramids from this period have long "causeways" leading from a so-called wally temple (near human dwellings) to the "mortuary temple". All pyramids have such "mortuary temples" attached to their sides. Again, Western appellations as "causeways," "valley temples," and "mortuary temples" may conceal more than they reveal about the purpose of these structures.

These long causeways were built like tunnels leading into the pyramid complex. When people engaged these tunnels bringing all their "offerings" they emerged into a court where the sun, in the form of a pyramidion, glittered above a shining white mega construction, only to be met by the "'dead" pharaoh housed as a statue in the "mortuary temple." There must be some symbolic significance to these arrangements. Western observers only see stones.

In Mankaure's "mortuary temple," Reisner found fragments of a larger-than-life statue of Menkaure that must have been the centerpiece of the temple. From here, the "King" could look across an open court through the entrance hall and down the long "causeway" to the human dwellings. Behind the statue at the back of the temple, at the base of the pyramid was a "false door." Significantly, the statue is placed so that the "King" seems to emerge from the inside of the pyramid through the door. He seems to be crossing the threshold between the inside and the outside of the pyramid (Lehner 1997: 136).

These are not merely archeological observations. These finds tell us things about a culturally constituted world. The door acted as a portal between the inner world of the pyramid and the outer world of ordinary life. Westerners only see a stone wall that looks like a door, so they call it a "false door." Western logic dictates that people cannot walk through stones. Whether this is possible or not is based on how "reality" and personhood are conceptualized in Ancient Egypt compared to in the West. Ancient Egyptians could walk through stones, or rather one part of their personhood could. This has everything to do with how personhood is understood in the two different eras and places in question. But never the twain shall meet, alas.

In practical terms, Mankaure ended the 4th Dynasty. None of his sons reached the throne. Instead, Shepseskaf became the new ruler, and he was from another family. For some reason, he chose to build a *mastaba*-like structure in South Saqqara. Maybe he did not have the genealogical credentials to build a pyramid. According to Manetho a new dynasty began after his passing (Lehner 1997: 140).

Pharaohs still built pyramids, but they were smaller and less skillfully constructed. But it was not economic hardship that caused the pyramids to shrink. Quite the contrary, it seems that Egyptian international trade blossomed in this period. During the reign of the first ruler of the 5th Dynasty, Userkaf, there is evidence of voluminous trade between the Aegean area and Egypt. His successor, Sahura even expanded Egypt's trade with its neighbors both in the Mediterranean and to the South. Large quantities of products were imported from tropical Africa. These included myrrh, gold, ivory, resins and leopard skins (Wenke 2009: 279).

Tellingly, Sahura's pyramid is called "The pyramid where the *ba* spirit rises." His successor's pyramid had a similar name: "The pyramid of the *ba* spirit." Another pyramid from this dynasty was called "The pyramid which is Devine of the *ba* spirit" (Vendel 2016c) (*ba* is not a spirit but a special part of Ancient Egyptian personhood. I shall return to this issue).

It also seems that the elite class expanded markedly in this period (Wenke 2009: 279). There is evidence that some elites grew richer, and they started to build large *mastabas* at Saqqara (Wenke 2009: 279). During the reign of each ruler of the 5th Dynasty, large enclosures for the sun god Re were also constructed. These structures had the same basic layout as the pyramid structures, but instead of a pyramid there was a granite obelisk (Lehner 1997: 150). This may be a kind of generalized pyramid form, perhaps built to serve a larger part of the population. It may also reflect a "democratization" of the ritual space to accommodate the increasing numbers of upper-class Egyptians.

Unas was the last ruler of the 5th Dynasty. At this time, Egyptian presence was marked in Byblos. Plenty of royal offerings were found in the temples in Byblos, amongst other things a vase from Unas. There was also a cylinder seal dated to 2350 BC that belonged to a totally Egyptianized Byblos prince, who apparently signed his documents with a seal incised with Egyptian hieroglyphs (Aubet 2013: 233).

The Unas pyramid is the smallest of all the Old Kingdom pyramids. Its splendor was kept inside. For the first time since Djoser, we see a highly decorated pyramid interior. It had the same layout as previous pyramids, but in the "burial" chamber was a black painted sarcophagus sunk partly into the floor. Around this, the walls were lined with alabaster incised and painted to represent a reed mat and wood frame enclosure mimicking the type of primitive shines used by the earliest Egyptians (Wilkinson 2010: 103). The ceiling was sprinkled with golden stars against a dark blue background which looked like the night sky (Wilkinson 2010: 102).

More importantly, the rest of the "burial" chamber, the "antechamber" and a section of the horizontal passage are covered with vertical columns of intricately carved hieroglyphs (Lehner 1997: 154), painted blue to symbolize the watery "Netherworld" (Wilkinson 2010: 103). It is nighttime and watery inside the pyramids; hence, pyramid interiors are clearly part of the "Netherworld."

These inscriptions are some of the earliest surviving texts from Ancient Egypt, but some of the texts are clearly much older (Wilkinson 2010: 103). These scripts are called "The Pyramid Texts," and they were to be repeated in subsequent pyramids. Not in identical renderings, but with more or less extensive extracts from a repertoire of texts concerning life and death. These "texts" must be seen as forerunners of "The Book of the Dead," that is, a long papyrus recounting the "deceased's" journey through the "Netherworld." These papyri were deposited in coffins, hence their English name.

In Ancient Egypt, however, these papyri had a completely different name. At that time, they were called "Going Forth by Day," giving an entirely different ontology to the text. Being dead is a far cry from "going forth by day." These different expressions clearly do not belong to the same cultural universe, and they do not share the same understanding of life and death.

These hieroglyphs are not randomly dotted throughout the pyramid. They clearly depict a movement through the pyramid (Allen 1994). From these hieroglyphs, it is possible to "read a pyramid" (Allen 1994). For the first time, we have a kind of manual for the pyramids, which explains what is going on inside them, and their purpose. To be able to read and understand the purpose of the pyramids, it is necessary to relate the story told inside them (Allen 1994) to Ancient Egyptian cosmology and its understanding of personhood.

From the number of Egyptian objects found in Byblos, the 5th Dynasty probably represents the climax of relations between Byblos and Egypt (Aubet 2013: 233). Both pharaohs Pepi I and II sent presents to Byblos. More than thirty-six Egyptian offerings from this period have been found there. These two pharaohs also raised a temple in Byblos, and Egyptian festivals were celebrated there. There was also a considerable colony of Egyptian specialists operating in Byblos, who organized different aspects of "trade" with Egypt (Aubet 2013: 234). It seems like a period with growing prosperity both for Byblos and Egypt.

At the same time in Egypt, the elite group was growing bigger and included more sections of society. It also seems that the pharaohs lost some of their power and that there was a certain decentralization of authority. Before Pepi II, the elite decorated their tomb walls with texts that celebrated their connections to the royal court. Now, the growing elite began to stress its own accomplishments (Wenke 2009: 280–1). A new class of artisans, craftsmen and specialists also gained influence and prosperity (Rice 1993: 222).

This development could signal a growing prosperity that was no longer appropriated solely by the Pharaoh. The expanding activities in Byblos could certainly support such a view, but by Egyptologists it is mostly see as a period of decadence and a loss of central power to corrupt regional administrators (Rice 1993: 220). Rice sees this development as wholly alien to the original social structure of the unified Kingdom (Rice 1993: 222–3).

According to this view, Ancient Egypt was imploding. However, sharing resources is not the same as general decline. Ultimate kingship is not the only way for a civilization to survive. Maybe Ancient Egypt was beginning to morph into something better than Divine Kingship and ultimate rule.

The Pharaohs kept building pyramids throughout the 6th Dynasty, and although they were on a smaller scale, they were splendidly decorated on the inside. In Pepi I's pyramid, these decorations covered a greater area of the walls than in previous pyramids. During its restoration, archeologists also found a pink granite canopic chest, with its lid still on, set into the floor niche in front of the sarcophagus. It contained fragments of alabaster jars. Close by, a tightly wrapped bundle was found containing a complete packet of viscera that had been in one of the jars–and which presumably belonged to Pepe I (Lehner 1997: 158).

Despite all the sealed and empty sarcophaguses found so far, this find shows that some parts of the dead pharaohs did find their way into pyramids. At the same time, the layout of the pyramids was further simplified. There was no longer any need for two or more rooms inside them. It seems that one central chamber was enough and that it both contained the sarcophagus and a canopic chest for the viscera (Khufu's so-called King and Queen's chamber in one?).

Pepe II was the last pharaoh of the 6th Dynasty. He also entertained close relations with Byblos. He became the longest ruling pharaoh. He lived for 100 years and according to Manetho he ruled for ninety-four of these years (Lehner 1997: 161). His pyramid is essentially the same as those immediately before him. It also had a single room containing a sarcophagus and a canopic chest.

Pepe II died in 2175 BC. A common description of this period, repeated over and over, is that

> towards the end of his reign, the central power was weak and out of means and local rulers so strong, that the government of Egypt simply collapsed. His two noted successors were merely puppets in the hands of the real rulers, and had no power whatsoever. (Vendel 2016d)

Pepi II was succeeded by his son Nemtyemsaf II, who in turn was succeeded by Neitiqerty Siptah. None of them ruled for very long (Wilkinson 2010: 119). State building came to a halt, as did foreign expeditions, and desert posts were abandoned. In the twenty years that followed, Egypt had seventeen "kings" (Wilkinson 2010: 119). An unknown "king" named Iti from this period sponsored an expedition to Wadi Hammamat to collect stones for a pyramid, but it was never built. One of the longest reigns at this time was that of Ibi who was in office for two years, one month and a day. He managed to build a pyramid. It had a core of mud, small stones and chips of limestone, but the outer casing was never started. It only reached a height of 18 m, the same size as the Pepi II queen pyramid (Wilkinson 2010: 121).

The pharaoh and the government were located in Memphite, but in an attempt to gain control, or perhaps to stay in office, a "pharaoh by title" who was called Neferirkara promoted a man called Shemai as governor of Upper Egypt and confirmed the successor for this office as his son Idy. The central authority had lost its sovereign power. From ruling a unified Egypt, the pharaohs had become dependent on the landed nobility of Upper Egypt (Wilkinson 2010: 122). Instead, the puppet pharaohs tried to use royal privileges to honor, or bribe, their supporters in Upper Egypt. This was, of course, the home of Egypt's main gold deposits.

However, Egypt's crisis was not generated internally, nor was it a local phenomenon. Egypt's main trading partner suddenly disappeared. Byblos's glory days ended with a great wave of burning and destruction that is evident both on the city wall and the temples. Contact with Egypt ended and would not be resumed until 12th Dynasty (Aubet 2013: 235). Concurrently, most of Western Syria experienced disruption. Excavated middle Khabur sites show they were deserted. Other sites were burned or abandoned, totally or partly (Akkermans and Schwartz 2003: 283).

At Tell Leilan in Syria, once called Shekhna which was once a provincial center commanding the Khabur River Valley, a massive building project was underway with walls two meters thick dressed from great basalt boulders brought to the site from at least 40 km away. Construction work seems to have stopped overnight, leaving basalt boulders in various stages of preparation. Urban life completely ceased everywhere. In Tell Brak nearby, the residents had withdrawn to huddle in a quarter of the former area (Kriwaczek 2010: 129).

Even Ur, the peak place of Sumerian achievement, experienced devastation. It fell to hordes of Gutians. This happened simultaneously with the Hurrians' and Amorites' move into North Syria, pushing south and east and causing the small city-states there to disintegrate (Crawford 2004: 219). Altogether, we see a massive collapse in the most important regions of Egyptian foreign export and import. No wonder there were also massive changes in Egypt. "By this time, the gods had gone from Egypt" (Rice 1993: 229), and "the system of royal government that had served Egypt for a millennium had come to an inglorious end" (Wilkinson 2010: 122). The Old Kingdom was over. Ancient Egypt had lost its momentum.

This description of crisis is seen from the rulers' perspective. It is, however, clear from the archeological data that a thriving culture existed among the poorer levels of society, and that intense social developments were taking place in the provincial towns of Upper Egypt (Shaw 2000: 110). For the next 200 years, there was to be no unified kingdom—and no more splendor for a long time to come. The following period is called "The First Intermediate Period."

The preceding account of Egyptian history as part of a larger trade network is largely conjectural. However, without such a larger perspective the ebb and flow of Egyptian society is almost inexplicable. What this perspective tells us is that Egypt's social organization and economy were mostly based on its ability to export gold, and that social conditions in Egypt were, to a large extent, a reflection of foreign demand for this product. Egypt's splendor was intimately related to its trading contacts with the surrounding world—all through the ages. The character of these relations determined the ep and flow of Egypt's social world.

There is no doubt that gold was in high demand in the ancient world, but it is very difficult to determine the origin of gold, and the fact that it can be melted repeatedly only complicates matters. However, had there been other major centers for gold prospecting, apart from Egypt, we would probably also have seen centers of accumulation and social differentiation in the regions in question, given the importance of gold in the reproduction of status and power both in the past and present.

From this revised narrative, it is clear that Egypt was the primary exporter of gold in the ancient world, and that this made it tremendously rich and able to build the world's largest constructions. Gold was also the major factor behind the different development trajectories of Upper and Lower Egypt. It was Upper Egypt that had access to gold, developed a steep social hierarchy, and built monumental structures. Not Lower Egypt. Lower Egypt were merely trading intermediaries between Upper Egypt and the East.

There is not a single shard of archeological evidence that it was the unification of Upper and Lower Egypt that gave rise to Ancient Egypt, as we know it. The Narmer palette must be telling a different story. Neither is there any evidence that the union of these "Two Lands" was brought about by violent means or any other form of subjugation. While we know the names of the Pre-dynastic rulers of Upper Egypt, there is no mention anywhere of any important ruler from Lower Egypt who could have been subjugated. There are simply no archeological finds that indicate large scale battle, there are no signs of *en masse* burial of fatally wounded people, and there are no weapons in the graves. It seems to have been a gradual process of incorporation as the two 'places' became increasingly integrated through trade.

One of the things that we do know for certain from this period is that the A-group in Nubia disappeared, possibly indicating that the area was integrated into the growing kingdom of Abydos. Abydos therefore became the sole proprietor of gold in the region. Instead of an insignificant integration of Upper and Lower Egypt, with no real economic potential, the expropriation of Nubia seems to have been the event that gave rise to the First Dynasty. As time went by, the arable land in the delta was useful to fill the pharaohs' coffers. Nothing more.

This exposition of Ancient Egyptian early history also seem to point to a particular Egyptian predilection for dividing social life into pairs, like in the "crowns" and "titles" of the pharaoh. Everything Egyptian seems to refer to something "double." As this exposition also suggests, this should not be taken as a reflection of some form of geo-politics involving "two lands."

Rather, I propose that the most important issue for Ancient Egyptians was their relationship to their gods, or in other words, their ancestors; and that the pharaoh was always regarded as the contemporary manifestation of the god Horus. All the Ancient Egyptians' magnificent buildings are about this relationship: enclosures, temples and pyramids.

In my view, it is most likely this relationship between humans and the gods that is at stake in their constant references to "two realms," "two lands," "two crowns," and double "titles." To understand this better, we must insert these symbols—crowns, titles, and lands—into Ancient Egyptian cosmology, and investigate the social system that underpinned this cosmology.

Chapter 2

Gold and Social Organization

Material conditions are never limited to the cultural group proper, they have to exchange with their surrounding and the resulting material condition have to be divided and organized in-between social groups. This means that a society have to exchange resources both with the surrounding world and internally between groups and individuals in society. This is a truism.

All through the ages, Ancient Egypt had exchange relations with the Levant and Mesopotamia, and with larger Africa with whom they exchanged various products: gold for prestige goods. Together these exchanges created the material foundation for the reproduction of Egyptian society.

In non-monetary societies' internal exchange relations, the relationship between groups, can only be expressed in kinship terms producing some form of kinship system that distributed resources between groups within society. Ancient Egyptian kinship system—if we are able to establish the configuration of this—would supply invaluable information about the material condition of the society, its social organization, and the special character and position of the pharaohs.

All social groups belong to larger networks based on kinship and the exchange of partners. Such lasting relationships have to be symbolically expressed. This is typically done through the exchange of prestige goods, objects needed for the special occasions that were important, imported over long distances—hence their role as prestige goods—otherwise everybody would have them and there would be no need to exchange them or use them to express status and social relationships (Bergendorff 2016).

As a result, kinship also carries the seed of social stratification. Social hierarchy and unequal exchange are a question of access to, the amount of, and the social restrictions associated with the prestige goods available (Bergendorff 2016). This issue is at the heart of the strategic game for social power.

To become a place of wonders and majestic buildings, Ancient Egypt needed large amounts of resources and access to prestige goods. Egypt must have had access to both, and its people must also have had a social organization that ensured their distribution in society. Without ways to amass resources and exchange some of these for prestige goods, and without ways for some groups to be able to monopolize these, there would be no social hierarchy or division of labor. There would only be homogenous groups.

There must be an explanation for Egypt's wealth and splendor, and this can only be its vast gold deposits which made it possible for some segments of society to become immensely rich. We know that the Badarian herders exploited the Eastern Desert for grazing land. The ethnographic material strongly suggests that the Wadis used for this were divided into groups according to their family lines. Some families had access and "ownership" over gold rich Wadis and others did not. Those who controlled the gold deposits were able to procure the all-important social prestige goods from far away. Those without access to gold would have had to exchange local products for prestige goods from those who had.

Over time, this would create a status hierarchy in Upper Egypt consisting of an internationally connected upper class and a locally producing lower class. In the end, this would have laid the foundation for the Old Kingdom, making the pharaohs immensely rich.

ANCIENT EGYPTIAN KINSHIP

Kinship does not leave many archeological traces, but we do know that Ancient Egyptian dynasties were solely based on family, that the pharaoh office was hereditary and that pharaohs occasionally married close kin. We also know that kinship is the primordial way of organizing resources between groups and therefore that it reflects the character of the social reproduction of a society (Bergendorff 2016). Hence, pharaohs were part of some kind of kinship system.

However, contrary to what many people think, it is not kinship or marriage that determines relations between groups. Instead, it is exchange or alliance relations that determine the distribution of kinship categories, which is just to say that kinship is not endogenous to groups but a result of the character of the exchange relations between groups.

Therefore, the kinship system in any one group is not an inherent feature of a local culture that can be studied on its own. It is all about relationships. This is demonstrated by the fact that kinship category terms such as mother's brother's daughter (MBD) are applied not just to real cousins, but to all appropriate members of a group that relate to one's own group as "wife-givers." Who you are supposed to marry has an immense influence on the resulting kinship system.

If we can determine which kinship system prevailed in Ancient Egypt, we will have a clearer picture of the relationship between groups and their social organization of resources. However, to date, most debate has centered on whether Ancient Egypt was organized along matrilineal lines so that descent and inheritance passed through the female line. Flinders Petrie seems to think so (1924), and so does Margaret Murray (1949). On the other hand, some think that Ancient Egypt was patrilineal and that inheritance passed through the male line, as argued by O'Connor and Reid (1990).

In support of the argument that Egypt was a matrilineal society, Petrie writes,

In questions of descent the female line was principally regarded. The mother's name is always given, the father's name may be omitted; the ancestors are always traced farther back in the female than in the male line. The father was only a holder of office; the mother was the family link. (Petrie 1924: 119)

Murray backs up this view, writing,

[Women] enjoyed a peculiar position from the fact that all landed property descended in the female line from mother to daughter. The entail in the female line seems to have been fairly strict, and nowhere so strict as in the royal family. (Murray 1949: 100)

In contrast, Forgeau, who believed that Ancient Egypt was patrilineal, writes,

[T]he rule of succession, from brother to brother until the branch became extinct, and from uncle to son of the eldest brother is further evidence of the greater importance attached to patrilinearity. (Forgeau in Allen 1996: 135)

This is backed up by O'Connor, who writes, "Historic Egypt was organized along partriarchal lines" (O'Connor 1990: 8). Kemp states that "the succession was patrilineal, i.e. father-son" (Kemp 1983: 219).

In short, we have some rather contradictory statements about kinship and linearity in Ancient Egypt. It is claimed that the father is only the holder of office, but that succession was from father to son, or from uncle to the son of the eldest brother, while landed property descended in the female line, and that women had great status. To complicate matters, we also know from so-called marriage contracts that the groom paid a price to the wife's family and that the father of the bride would contribute domestic goods and food to the new household (Allen 2009: 31): Such a contract may read:

I have taken you as a wife. I have given you (sum of "money" listed here) as your *shep en sehemet*. If I repudiate you as a wife, be it that I hate you, be it that

I want another woman as a wife instead of you, I shall give you (sum of money is here listed apart from (sum of money listed) which I have given you as your *shep en shemet*. (Allen 2009: 31)

This "contract" is from a later period but it nonetheless establishes the fact that paying bride price was a common practice, probably throughout the ages. For sure, bride price was not paid in "money" but in some form of prestige goods. This means that bride price travelled from the groom's family to the wife's family while a form of tribute in domestic goods traveled from the wife's family to the groom.

Furthermore, some pharaohs married their sisters, who thereby became the mothers of the heirs to the throne (Dodson and Hilton 2004: 16). Such practices were obviously also part of the Ancient Egyptian kinship system. It is often argued that the social justification for such marriages must have sprung from the mythological couplings of sibling deities such as Osiris and Isis, where Isis is both sister and wife to Osiris. His brother Seth killed him, and then Osiris and Isis had a son, Horus, who is always the present pharaoh. This explanation suggests that practices emulate mythology, essentially assuming that someone has to think up a practice that is not yet practiced so that the living can do it! This is plainly improbable. So-called mythology must be rooted in social reality, or it would be mere prattle to real-life inhabitants.

Linking kinship to the social reproduction of Pre-Dynastic or Ancient Egypt would solve the apparent conundrums of Egyptian kingship. It would also help us to explain "Divine Kingship" and the Egyptian predilection for dualism, instead of just stating that these are results of a particular Egyptian mindset. To the untrained, all these seemingly contradictory elements may seem difficult to reconcile. However, a trained anthropologist immediately recognizes that these are all elements of the kinship system known as *matrilateral cross cousin marriages with avuncular residence*.

In this system, "a man" marries his mother's brother's daughter and goes to live with her. So he is basically living at his uncle's place, since the latter married into that residence in the previous generation. This explains the fact that the succession passed from the uncle to the son of the eldest brother. Uncles and sons lived in the same residence.

To illuminate the special character of such a kinship system and the way it organizes resources, we must relate it to kinship systems in general. According to Jonathan Friedman (who taught me all about this), there are only three basic forms of kinship system; all others are derivatives of these. Kinship is based on exogamy and the exchange of women and this situation divides the primary sibling group (brothers and sisters) into two groups: those who "leave" and those who "stay."

Therefore, the rule of exogamy requires that males and females pursue different marital careers. As a logical extension of this, exogamy also divides cousins into what are known as parallel and cross cousins, that is, parallel cousins are those children who are related through siblings of the same sex as the father's brother's children (FBch), and those related through the mother's sister's children (MZch). On the other hand, cross cousins are those related through siblings of the opposite sex through the father's sister's children (FZch) and those related though the mother's brother's children (MBch), and this applies to second, third, and all other cousins. This means that parallel cousins belong to the same unilinear grouping as siblings, while cross cousins belong to a separate unilinear grouping, that is, the one into which one can marry. Schematically, it looks like this:

//	x			x	//
male;	female;	marriage;	siblings;	parallel cousins;	cross cousins

This illustrates that parallel and cross cousins live in separate locations, and serve different purposes in the overall kinship structure. As a direct result of the different marital careers of sisters and brothers and the implications this has for the distribution of cousins between groups, it is the intergroup relations that determine which cousins one can marry. Cousin relationships therefore translate directly into exchange relations, and there are three forms of cross-cousin marriages—bilateral, matrilateral, and patrilateral—which correspond to three elementary structures of exchange: restricted exchange, generalized matrilateral exchange, and generalized patrilateral exchange, in which patrilateral exchange produces short exchange cycles while matrilateral exchange produces long exchange cycles.

In bilateral cross-cousin marriage, Father and Mother's Brother live in two different groups and simply exchange sisters. Their relationship is based on reciprocity between two groups, and therefore the exchange system is restricted to these two groups. In patrilateral cross-cousin marriage, one marries one's Father's Sister's Daughter (FZD). When one marries one's FZD, one marries a woman from the group into which one's FZ married, which implies taking a woman from a group to which one's own group gave a woman in the previous generation. Consequently, the flow of women is reversed in each generation (most egalitarian).

Neither of these two forms of kinship system allows for the creation of hierarchies. This is a result of the resource distribution in the area where such kinship systems are practiced. And neither of these systems is relevant in the Egyptian case. Such systems may have existed here in the remote past, but at some point they must have changed into a matrilateral cross-cousin marriage system, because in such systems the groups are in permanent relationship with each other either as wife-givers or wife-takers. Depending on the resource situation, this can turn into a hierarchical relationship.

In matrilateral cross-cousin marriage, one marries one's Mother's Brother's Daughter (MBD) and she will come from the same group, as the group one's Mother came from, that is, one's MB's group. This does not imply reciprocity but a one-way exchange of women between groups, so that the same group will always be wife-givers to the same group. This implies long cycles of exchange, and at least three groups, so that one's MB and MBS can also find wives, or else problems will arise at both ends of the exchange systems. Ancient Egypt is one of many empirical examples of this. Schematically, it looks like this:

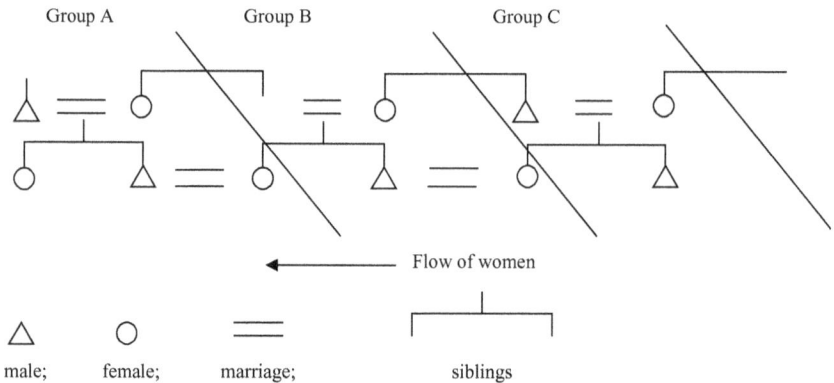

Matrilateral cross-cousin marriage with avuncular residence is a special case of this more common matrilateral cross-cousin marriage system in that it introduces a residential component. We find such kinship systems in historical centers of power in Central Africa such as the Kongo Kingdom. Therefore, to gain a better understanding of Ancient Egyptian kinship systems and social organization, we must investigate how they worked in the African Kongo Kingdom (this kingdom collapsed soon after European contact in the mid-seventeenth century) (Friedman 2008: 233–4).

In relation to the debate about Ancient Egypt being a matri- or patrilineal society, material from West Africa suggests that these categories are not quite as significant as they have been made out to be (Leach 1961). This is especially clear from the ethnography of the Kongo Kingdom. Congo-type societies like the Kongo Kingdom from this period have traditionally been regarded as matrilineal societies because the micro-unit consisted of so many matrilineal descent groups and therefore it was assumed that the macro group had the same structure as its constituent parts (Friedman 2008: 236).

However, as Ekholm Friedman argues, we must reverse this causality between micro- and macro- group levels and look at how the macro group as such consists both of specific subgroups and a structure which unites them, lending an internal dynamic to the system as a whole. In this macro system, we have kinship-based subunits and a political structure that unites them. The latter is intimately related to the possibility of accumulating the prestige goods necessary for the social reproduction of individuals, since these are used for bride price and also enable the elders to establish and maintain dominance over the younger members of society (Friedman 2008: 231–6).

In the Kongo Kingdom system, groups sent out their sons to be married in sub-clans to which they paid bride price, and who in turn sent their sons off to be married in another sub-clan where they paid bride price, and in every instance, this was reciprocated through some kind of tribute. Sons were sent out to marry their mother's brother's daughters (MBD). This meant that the same group was in a constant position as wife-giver to the same recipient group across generations. It also meant that women, so to speak, married upward in the system and were accompanied by tribute, while prestige goods traveled in the other direction, giving tribute and redistribution of equivalent but different products (Friedman 2008: 244). Schematically it looks like this:

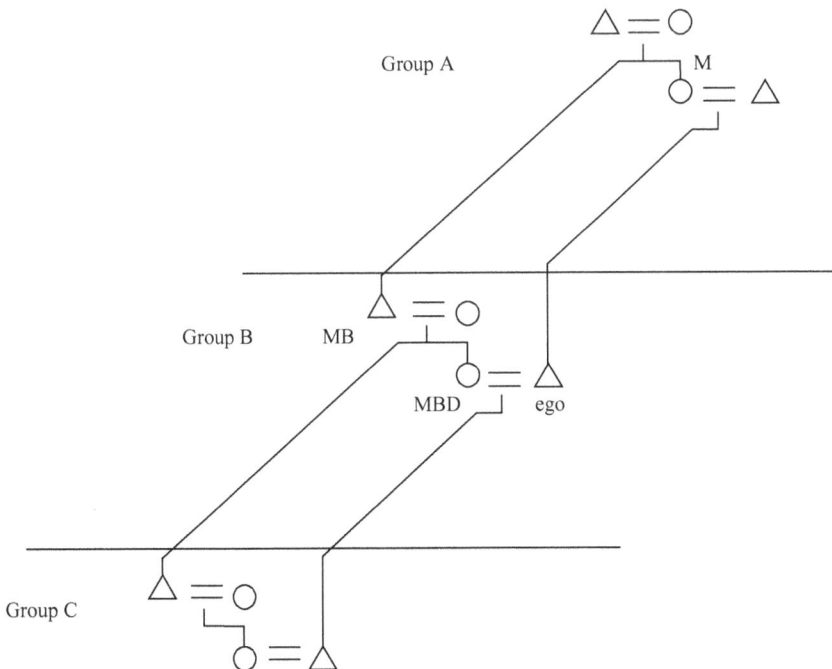

As a curiosity, it seems that Ancient Egypt reverted to such a system later during the twelfth dynasty. This is not surprisingly, since this system is eminently suited to distribute resources and prestige goods between the wealthy classes. In the tombs of Twelfth Dynasty monarchs in Middle Egypt offer evidence of such a system having existed, indicating that the political structure was probably organized this way again at this time (leaving out the First Intermediate Period).

At this time, Khnumhotep II reigned in the sixteenth nome (nome being a province in Ancient Egypt). His mother had married a man called Nehri from the Fifteenth Nome. In addition, Khnumhotep's eldest son Nakht was appointed governor of the adjacent Seventeenth Nome, thus linking at least these three nomes by kinship (Lloyd 2014: 163–5). This clearly indicates that men moved to live with their wives, producing local matrilineages and regional patrilineages.

It is also clear that with the development of the Egyptian state, the royal family did not have the means or personal to conduct all the affairs of state, building temples, pyramids, wage war, and look into all the petty daily affairs of state government. So evidently, there were changes to this kinship-based system. Bureaucracy came to play a bigger role. "With the expansion of the pharaonic administration, the highest officials were no longer sought from the males of the royal house" (Spalinger 2013).

Still, in both the Congo and Egyptian cases, we see that the appearance of local matrilineal groups was the result of a political structure in which men moved out, producing a power structure that integrated the whole system. As Ekholm Friedman writes, "The localized segment of the matrilineage . . . has, in fact, no independent structural existence" (2008: 236).

Consequently, the question of matrilinearity versus patrilinearity is dependent on how kinship relates to local resource exploitation and on the possible presence of prestige goods that can be exchanged for tribute in intergroup relations. Such systems appear to have both matri- and patrilineal elements depending on which way you look at it. In such systems, inheritance is passed from father to son, irrespective of whether or not they live together. Men are office holders, despite women being landholders. This is the reason for the abovementioned confusion about Ancient Egypt's kinship system.

In such systems, some inbuilt problems arise at the top and at the bottom of the system (which are evident in the above schema). At the very top of the hierarchy, the lineage can only be a wife-taker, because there are no higher groups to which they can give their daughters. In consequence, this group retains its own women (Friedman 2008: 244), or is compelled to send them out of the system, to a non-related society. There is a similar problem at the bottom of the system where in order to survive as an independent group they must find someone that their sons can marry, or else they will be incorporated into a higher ranking group (Friedman 2008: 244).

Ancient Egypt seems to have faced the same kind of problem. One solution to the problem at the top is to marry your sister, as happened in some instances. Such marriages were therefore a result of the kinship system and not a way of mimicking the storylines of myths (cf. above). Instead, the story about Osiris, Isis, Seth, and Horus for instance, should be seen as an account of the contradictions in the kinship system.

In these systems, exchange takes place between the involved groups in which tribute is paid "upward" in the system towards wife-givers, while equivalent but different products flow downwards. Men marry downward in the system, paying bride price, which in Ancient Egypt was called *shep en sehemet* (translated as compensation for marrying a women: Allen 2009: 31), which was paid in prestige goods in return for tribute.

Relations between superiors and inferiors were not symmetrical. There is only one group at the top, but it can and does have relations with several inferior groups. To be able to send products to all their wife-givers in return for tribute, the highest-ranking group must produce accordingly, and this is repeated at each level. The highest-ranking group cannot simply return its vassals' articles, because this would end the relationship.

All groups probably produced local products on an equal footing, therefore the highest-ranking group would have had to have some product that made them appear economically stronger. They may have had access to much-needed prestige goods, but they would also have needed a local product that could be exchanged for such external products. This makes it vital to control some form of natural deposit as a source for obtaining external prestige goods (Friedman 2008: 246). All the centers of power in Central Africa were located near natural sources of prestige items like copper, salt, and shells.

Such Kongo-type structures, and by extension also Ancient Egypt, cannot exist in a closed space. They need an exterior world (Friedman 2009: 246). If the external source of prestige goods disappears or the local source dries up, the highest-ranking group loses its means of existence. As we have seen, this is exactly what happened during the so-called First Intermediate Period: Egypt's external world collapsed, and it lost its connection to its trading partners in Byblos.

In Ancient Egypt, gold was arguably the prestige item that made extraordinary hierarchies possible. Gold was the means for the highest-ranking groups to exchange foreign prestige goods that could be used to pay off their vassals.

This is the reason why all the major centers—Hierakonpolis, Naqada, Abydos, and Nubia—were located near gold deposits.

Introducing kinship into the study of Ancient Egypt brings a new dimension that can explain many hitherto puzzling phenomena. Suddenly, Ancient Egyptian practices are no longer a result of a special Egyptian mindset but an expression of an underlying kinship system that organized the distribution of resources.

From later material from West Africa, we can now see why Ancient Egypt showed both matri- and patrilineal characteristics, and why women possessed landed property while men were office holders. Landed property passed down the female line while political offices passed down the male lineages, producing a system of local matrilineages and dispersed regional patrilineages that integrated the system. To function, such systems need a natural deposit that could be used to exchange prestige goods with a foreign partner.

All societies in historic West Africa recognized both matrilineal and patrilineal elements. This combination of matri- and patrilineality gives rise to a corresponding duality in the political and ideological structure. Kinship—or rather its inherent dualism—is elevated to ideology or "myth," if you will. In some places, such dualisms find their expression in an idea that society consists of two ethnic strata, an original matrilineal population and a younger patrilineal conquering group. In the Kongo Kingdom, such a dualism found its expression in a myth about a king sending his son out to conquer and occupy new land. In reality, this "migration" was repeated in every generation, depicted as the patrilineage "conquering" the local population.

Such an ideology leads us straight back to one of the most consistent images from Ancient Egypt—one that is so consistent throughout the ages that it cannot be based on any "real" event. In Ancient Egypt, a myth akin to that of the (similarly organized) Kongo Kingdom seems to have existed about a (patrilineal) "king" conquering his (matrilineal) enemies, which expressed the duality between the political structure and the landowning families. In other words, political office versus means of production.

In Egyptological parlance, this situation is depicted as the pharaoh doing something to a kneeling man which by Egyptologists is called "smiting the enemy" (be a visual expression for the "Kings" close connection to the source for prestige good). Often, these enemies take the form of unidentified "Westerners." Yet this scene might more plausibly be seen as the transformation of a kinship system into ideology. In every generation, the king sent out his sons to "conquer" the localized matrilineages. That event is a result of the conditions that a *matrilateral cross-cousin marriage with avuncular residence* system would impose on social reality. Such an imaginary could also be extended to Egyptian trading partners who supplied the necessary prestige goods.

And indeed, the scene in question does not seem to depict straightforward aggression. The "King" and the one being smitten seem, rather, to be ceremoniously engaged with each other—both are holding onto some form of fabric and a box that is pressed against the forehead of the kneeling person, who is holding on to the leg of the "King." This may be a way to illustrate that the "King" is the source of the all-important "life-force" of the group (prestige goods).

Chapter 3

Ancient Egyptian Cosmology

Historically, we have seen that Ancient Egypt's splendor relied on its vast gold resources that were located in different Wadis leading into the Nile valley. These deposits were located in places that the first Badarian herders used as grassing land for their cattle. From an early date, these grassing areas were probably divided into family plots, so that some families had access to the rich gold deposits while others did not. Those groups with gold deposits could then trade with surrounding areas, and thereby import and monopolize the much needed prestige goods that were used to mark social events locally. These imports and their monopolization are widely attested to in sumptuous graves, especially in Upper Egypt where the gold deposits were located. But these graves were only for the few, showing emergent differences in wealth and status.

By exchanging gold for foreign-produced prestige goods, Ancient Egypt became integrated into a much larger "international" trading system, stretching from deep within Africa, via Nubia, to the Levant and further on to Mesopotamia and beyond. In Egypt, these imported prestige goods were traded, or exchanged internally, for local products. This situation gave rise to a social system based on a small, internationally connected group with access to prestige goods, and local producers living off the land. Exchange between these two segments of society created the foundation for a division of labor and an immense difference in status between the two groups.

As in all pre-industrial societies, such exchange relationships could only be negotiated, or expressed, through some form of kinship system. And the only known kinship system relevant for the situation in Ancient Egypt (and which is also found in other parts of Africa in similar situations) is a *matrilateral cross-cousin marriage with avuncular residence.*

In such systems, the son moves out to live with his wife at her place of residence, where his uncle is already living, having married into this group in the previous generation. The uncle therefore has local authority over the "son" due to his seniority, but the "son" can still be the heir to the throne when that time comes.

In this kind of kinship system, the wife's group are landowners, to whom the out-marrying "son" pays bride price consisting of foreign, imported prestige goods. The local landowners are thereby integrated into a centralized political structure based on socially necessary prestige goods. In return for the prestige goods, the local group sends tribute in the form of local products to the groom's family, producing a situation based on unequal exchange of foreign prestige goods for local products.

Pre-dynastic and Ancient Egypt remained kinship-based societies throughout the ages. Kinship is not (as many believe) an inherent cultural quality of a society; rather, it expresses the character of the relationships between groups in a society. In turn, these relationships inform the character of social reality.

People do not just live out the properties of their social systems; they also have to make sense of the system they live within. They have to negotiate the properties of their social world, and these are not necessarily self-explanatory, but can have unresolvable and contradictory elements that also have to be negotiated. This result in the phenomenon we call "culture." Culture is not something people have, but something they do.

This is exactly where the problems start. In kinship-based societies, social relations are personal and cannot be rendered in abstract forms such as economics, politics, and so on. Therefore, the resulting social characteristics are often negotiated in (long) stories based on human (like) actors. Some call these stories "narratives." Westerners, who often do not understand the content of these stories, even if they are trained anthropologists, call them "myths." These same people call the practices associated with such stories "rituals" because seen from a Western perspective these practices have no effects in "the real world."

Since kinship-based societies have different categories than those Westerners deem "real," these societies appear to mix incompatible things, seen from a Western viewpoint. For instance, kinship-based societies do not distinguish between living and dead matter. Therefore, kinship-based societies appear immersed in myth, magic and rituals, at least seen from a Western point of view (non-religious Westerners cannot explain how "life" can spring from "dead" matter, but this is a problem created by Western categories).

Many anthropologists are skeptical of such characterizations of other societies. Skorupski points out that a so-called ritual statement cannot simply be translated because this would imply that identical meanings could be expressed in different linguistic forms (1976: 14). Meaning, he argues, is generated in a context, and

> the overall framework provides the indispensable, culturally shared categories within which a person understands his world. (1976: 227)

Tambiah is also very critical, cautioning us that by

> simply naming rituals of non-Western societies as "magic" and the substances used as "medicines" and "drugs," one cannot thereby attribute to the phenomena so named, by virtue of that naming, characteristic that may be peculiar to one's own contemporary civilisation. (1990: 357)

Reality is a social construct everywhere. Every group and social system has its own categories and related practices. Here, we are not just dealing with different representations of the same basic "objective natural" reality, but with differently constituted existential systems. Cross-culturally, there is no such thing as "nature." It is the Western belief in nature, as a universal material and unspiritual world, that make other people's categories stand out as "religious," which is just another Western "belief." This is tautological reasoning.

For Ancient Egyptians (and for many other cultures) "nature" simply does not exist. This means taking on board the fact that Egyptian expressions and stories are statements about *their* reality. To call these statements "myths" is a *characterization*, not an explanation. Using Western categories to characterize foreign societies makes it seem as though ancient peoples (and non-Western cultures) lived in fantasy worlds where their symbolic constructions appeared out of thin air, but nevertheless dominated their daily activities.

However, so-called mythology and myths cannot be free-standing fantasies based on their own universe. They have to relate to social reality as experienced by those who live in it, and who tell "stories" about it. Otherwise these "stories" would not make sense. And the natives themselves, the ones telling the stories, would be in the same position as later observers wondering about the meaning of these strange "stories." Let us instead try to see these "stories" as reflections of the social reality of the people in question, and to understand them in accordance with the way *they* conceived of their world— their cosmology.

Egyptian notions about the cosmos and its creation must necessarily conform to the properties and character of their social world. Therefore, Egyptian creation "stories" should not be regarded as mythology but as ideology. The so-called gods cannot do something that contravenes the social order. They have to conform to social reality just like everybody else. These narratives are not haphazard stories.

ANCIENT EGYPTIAN WORLDVIEW

In societies where people depend on personal relationships for their social reproduction, "abstract" forces like politics and economics cannot exist. In such societies, acts takes place in a family based organization and the influences or forces that impede on these can also only be represented in a personal form as the work (or as properties) of significant ancestors.

From the earliest days of Egypt, there must have been a notion about what Westerners call "genesis" and fate of human life. We do not know how this was conceptualized at the beginning of Pre-Dynastic Egypt because there are no written records from this time. We know how these issues were explained later on, and these explanations presumably built on previous conceptions.

A word of caution: translating old Egyptian texts is difficult, and understanding the meaning they convey more so. We are not only dealing with a phenomenally long-time span but also with the problem of connecting different ontologies in which the basic categories of existence, reality, and being are very different. To complicate matters even further, we have no living informants to clear up our doubts.

As Tyldesley rightly points out:

> All our stories (from Ancient Egypt] have to be read through the eyes of a translator who has to supply not only the words but also the underlying sentiments, subtleties, and nuances that will make that story accessible to a modern reader [*sic*]. It seems unlikely, however hard we try, that we will ever reach a full understanding of Egypt's literature. (2011: 10)

Still, she characters the stories that are so hard to translate as "fictional tales" (2011: 9), deriving "from a mixture of overlapping genres including myths, rituals, recitations, hymns, and magical spells" (2011: 11). Thus, she describes Ancient Egyptian practices according to "characteristics that may be peculiar to one's own contemporary civilizations" (Tambiah 1990: 357).

Instead we have to realize that in a kinship-based society "the world" *can* only be narrated in personal terms (if you choose to call this a religiously constituted universe, so be it). As Frankfort observes, "if the universe is animated, it is best understood in terms of human life" (2000 [1948]: 28).

We also have to realize that immanent social properties, that is, the qualities of things, objects, and beings and the surrounding world, were depicted in personalized form and in line with the Egyptians' own categorical system (which in no way resembled the Western system). Unfortunately, they did not leave behind any comprehensive handbook to explain these matters. They did, however, leave a lot of scattered texts that can shed light on these issues.

We encounter the problem of meaning immediately when trying to interpret the cosmology of the Ancient Egyptians for, as Assmann writes, "[t] he ancient Egyptian language has no word for 'religion'" (2001: 1). If the ancient Egyptians did not have a word for "religion," they probably did not have a word for "god" either, as these appellations are closely connected.

To understand the Egyptian notion of "creation" as more than just "fictional stories," we need to look into a more fundamental level of Egyptian cosmology, that is, how they perceived their surrounding world and its constitution. At the most fundamental level, Ancient Egyptians experienced their universe as being "alive from end to end" (Frankfort 2000 [1948]: 4).

Within a religious framework, Assmann calls such an experience of the world "divine presence" (2001: 6). He continues, "the entire land was believed to be symbolically inhabited by the gods" (2001: 18). "Symbolically" is of course a *characterization*—and not an explanation at all.

Still, Assmann's characterization conveys an image of a world with a conceptual system than differs from Western systems. Living in a world that is alive through and through means that everything has an invisible dimension that makes it alive, and which is thought to reside in "everything": people, animals, plants, stones, and rocks. This something is what Westerners usually call gods.

But

[w]hen the universe is not seen as dead matter, but as suffused with life, man's own existence—with the critical phases of birth, procreation, and death—imparts significance to the cosmic phenomena and acquires a new depth in return. (Frankfort 2000 [1948]: 28)

This also means that Egyptian so-called gods could not be the Ancients way or representing what Westerners perceive as natural phenomena. They simply did not have this category. For instance, in Ancient Egypt, plants did not just grow; they were induced to grow by some unseen internal force (usually called Osiris).

Ancient Egyptian texts are full of descriptions of their worldview and the role played by their so-called gods. These beings could reside in anything and everything. They were the force behind the observable world.

However, also seen through a religious framework, Frankfort makes the relevant observation that some form of divine (*sic*) command "had established the world in all its features, once and for all" (2000 [1948]: 24). For that reason, the "divine" force could take residence in everything:

He [Path the first ancestor according to the Memphite Theology] made their bodies (statues) resemble that which pleased their hearts (that is, the form in which they desired to be manifest). And so the gods entered into their bodies of every kind of wood, of every kind of stone, of every kind of clay, of every kind of thing which grow upon him, in which they have taken form (Frankfort 2000 [1948]: 24)—explanations in brackets are by Frankfort.

As Frankfort further notes, "There were many gods and . . . they were immanent in nature" (2000 [1948]: 25) (for a moment take no notice of the phrases "gods" and "nature" these categories are merely superimposed on Ancient reality).

Apart from the fact that the "divine" force can reside in everything, observe also the phrase "of everything which grows upon him," which is upon Path (the world), here portrayed as a living entity. Even the disc of the sun, the actual heavenly body before everyone's eyes, could not be conceived as a purely physical phenomenon, "since such a conception was simply unknown to the ancients" (Frankfort 2000 [1948]: 25). There was no nature, biology or physics.

If we ignore for a moment the religious tenor of Frankfort's writings, he nevertheless describes the ancient world in quite appropriate terms. Although he focusses on the personal characteristics he thought the "gods" had, he describes the ancient worldview in adequate (if slightly misleading) terms:

> [The gods] [t]hey personify power but remain incomplete as personages. And yet these vague and grandiose gods were not distant and intangible; the Egyptians lived forever within the sphere of their activities. Moreover, he comprehended these activities to a large extent in terms of human existence. (Frankfort 2000 [1948]: 28)

Therefore, in Ancient Egypt, the daily course of the sun was interpreted according to a human life cycle. Every morning, the sun was (re)born only to die (again) in the evening (Frankfort 2000 [1948]: 29). Mixing Western and Egyptian conceptual systems, Frankfort continues:

> The life of man, as individual and even more as a member of society, was integrated with the life of nature (*sic*). (2000 [1948]: 29)

In other words, they simply conceived of the universe in a different way from Westerners. Anyway, many of the so-called gods had life cycles, as exemplified by the sun which was born, flourished, and died every day. So the sun's character changed during its "life-time," giving "it" several qualities during its course of existence, not to mention the time-span during which the "sun" could not be observed. This partly observable "entity" obviously also had a hidden, invisible "night-time" identity.

So-called gods, considered individual "deities," might, like the sun called Re, be divided into several aspects of the same being (Tyldesley 2011: 20).

This is where all the fun starts. It is marvelous, confusing, and confounding. There seem to be no limits to the ways the Ancient Egyptians conceived of their "gods." They come in all shapes and sizes. For instance, Amun-Re's (the first living creature) was thought to have all-pervading powers. Frankfort then advises us to be cautious in interpreting old Egyptian lore, and practices.

Most of the time, we are simply presented with all kinds of strange creatures that could take on many forms and had several aliases. This is presumably in order to account for different aspects of their beings. To represent all these aspects, they could also unite to form composite or syncretized forms (Tyldesely 2011: 20). They could, for instance, be depicted as consisting of different body parts, or partly or wholly in animal forms, or even as a brick with a human head, as the goddess Meskhenet sometimes is (Tyldesley 2011: 21).

Hathor, for instance, appears as a woman with a cow's head, as a woman with a human face but with cow's ears, or as a complete cow. To make her representations even more complicated she can also appear as a snake, a lioness, or as a tree that is able to feed the king because it has breasts. "Gods" were not confined to a single mode of existence. They appeared as the whim took them, in any of their known manifestations (here we get the first insight into how complicated it is to understand pharaoh "titles" which consists of multiple entities).

These pictorial descriptions of "gods" are clearly not realistic portraits of gods as real living beings (but who are we to know?). They can look very different from scene to scene, in contrast to depictions of human beings who all tend to look very similar (Tyldesley 2011: 21).

However, when the "gods" were depicted in human form, there had to be some way of distinguishing who they were so that they did not just appear as an impersonal picture of anybody. Their special characteristics had to be shown in their particular context. The Egyptians probably did not intend their hybrid forms to represent some kind of mysterious reality that only they knew about.

"The designs were probably pictograms, not portraits" (Frankfort 2000 [1948]: 12). Therefore, we must assume that the animal features helped distinguish the "gods" and the role they played on different occasions, when these were conveyed in art form. Just like the different "crowns" on the heads of pharaohs in different "pictures." These "crowns" were also pictograms, which explained the role of the Pharaoh on different occasions.

Using animal features to help characterize "gods" may not be that strange. Animal species show a kind of permanence and a form of static reality. As species, animals never change, seen from the perspective of the Ancient Egyptians. As such, they share the powers that were attributed to Egyptian "gods" (Frankfort 2000 [1948]: 18). Animals therefore seem to share the fundamental nature of creation and belong to an everlasting sphere of existence that humans could only hope to partake in after death.

Some "gods" also switched between being visible and invisible, for instance by being visible at daytime and disappearing into another realm at night. Especially Re and Thoth, the sun and the moon, both show clear signs of repeated life cycles, and perform a recurrent disappearing act. Still, Egyptians could see their "gods." In this way, the "gods" were not distant, or abstract. Everybody could see Re move across the heavens and disappear. And the moon changed shape during the course of a month.

There was apparently a hidden dimension of existence. Some phenomena are clearly visible, some are not. Accordingly, the world is divided into sections. This division of the world into two realms is quite clear in Egyptian texts.

For instance in the *Book of the Night*, we follow Re through his daily routine:

> Emerging from the netherworld. Sitting in the morning-barque. Traversing the primeval ocean in the hour of the day "That Beholds the Perfection of Her Lord." Transforming into Khepri, Rising to the horizon. Entering the mouth. Emerging from the vulva. Shining in the gateway of Light-land in the hour "That Makes the Perfection of Re Shine." To create the sustenance of humankind. Of cattle and all the serpents, he has created. (Assman 2001: 106)

Re (the sun) had four "identities"—appearances. Three for daytime, here translated as "Light-land"; and one for nighttime, in this text translated as "Netherworld." In another text, concerning Osiris (the so-called "king" of the Netherworld), the dichotomy between the realms of "the world" is spelled out as follows: "You are radiant in Light-land. You endure in the Land of Enduring" (Assman 2001: 126). During Re's passage in Light-land he changed his name and his form: "Khepri in the morning, Re at midday, Atum in the evening" (Assmann 2001: 107).

These multiple "identities" were also represented differently. Re started out as a child called Khebri, who was depicted as a scarab beetle. Then, as an adult, he was depicted as Re, a falcon-headed man, and as an old man he was depicted as Atum, a ram-headed man (Assmann 2001: 107). In some texts (e.g., the *Book of the Underworld*), seventy-four different nocturnal versions of Re are listed (Tyldesley 2011: 77). Some records show that when Khepri died every night, he was dismembered and buried; and every morning he was reborn as good as new (Tyldesley 2011: 43).

It is clear from these extracts that the Egyptians considered "the world" a living organism, a notion that is vividly expressed in their conception of Re' travel around the world. He was "Entering the mouth," "emerging from the vulva" (of Nun, another "god") and he was circumnavigating "the world" in a barque, "sailing on the 'primeval ocean' that seemingly surrounded and connected the 'Light-land,' and the 'Netherworld'" (also called the "World of Endurance").

The Egyptians clearly contemplated the character of these two realms of existence. They had concepts for each, *nehen* for the visible world, and *djet* for the invisible world. According to Assmann, there has been considerable speculation among Egyptologists about how to understand these concepts. Since they seem to involve some kind of "temporality," most endeavors have focused on translating their meaning according to a Western notion of "time," and on interpreting their religious meaning (Assmann 2001: 74). There are references to these terms in the *Book of the Dead* (or *Going forth by Day*) in which "all beings" were explained as *neheh* and *djet*.

Since these two concepts characterize the two spheres of existence, it is not surprising that in Egyptian thought they represented the whole of reality (Assmann 2001: 74). Assmann therefore suggests that these concepts should be translated as "change" (*neheh*) and "completeness" (*djet*). These concepts have also been used when a deceased was about to enter into the plenitude of cosmic time. He was greeted with the words:

You unite with *neheh*-time, when it rises as the morning sun and with *djet*-time when it sets as the evening sun. (Assmann 2001: 75)

This is further elaborated upon in "The Book of the Dead" (Going Forth by Day), in which we read from the *Papyrus of Ani*:

Who is he? As for what exists, that means his injury [Osiris/Ani's dismemberment]. *Otherwise said*: That means his corpse. *Otherwise said*: It means eternity and everlasting. As for eternity, it means daytime; as for everlasting, it means night. (Goelet, Faukner, Andrews, Gunther, and Wasserman 2015: Plate 7-B)

Here we have a distinction between "eternity—daytime," eternity being a movement into the future, juxtaposed with "everlasting—night," everlasting meaning permanence, represented by *nehen—djet*.

According to Assmann, this division of the cosmos is also reflected in the relationship between two of the major "gods" of Ancient Egypt: Re and Osiris. Re as the changing god of light (visible), and Osiris the unchanging god of death in the Netherworld (nowhere to be seen).

Osiris was, then, the "god" of "the *djet* aspect of time," as Assmann calls it. He was even sometimes called *djet*, or Yesterday—that is, that which has taken form. He also bore the epithet "Wennefer," meaning "he who remains matured" (Assmann 2001: 78).

In contrast, Re was always in the process of becoming. With his endless rising and setting, he was the "god" of the *neheh* aspect of time/life.

According to the Ancients, these two "gods" who represented aspects of life, did not represent alternatives in relation to each other. "They were what they were only in relation to each other. Only the two together yielded reality" (Assmann 2001: 78).

In "The Book of the Dead" (*Going Forth by Day*), we read about the relationship between Osiris and Re: "*What does it mean?* As for yesterday, that is Osiris. As for tomorrow, that is Re" (Faulkner and Goelet 2015: Plate 7-A).

Night after night, Re would venture forth into the Netherworld, having taken on the form of a so-called *ba*, and around midnight he would unite with Osiris, the corpse that he belonged to but which lay motionless in the Netherworld (because he had been killed by his brother Set)—his so-called *ka*. This reunion ensured the continuity of the cosmos.

According to Assmann, life was conceived as a union of *ba* and corpse (*ka*). *Neheh* and *djet*. The visible and invisible parts of existence thus permeated the whole of Ancient existence. Everything, every object, every phenomenon, could be and was the abode of a "god." These objects were seen as living representations of (partly invisible) "gods," linking the Netherworld, the world of endurance with the Light-world of transient human bodies.

Such existential properties were the fundamentals of the Egyptian worldview. So far, these properties are not all that different from the ones we find in some contemporary kinship-based societies. There is nothing exceptional. Just like in these societies, we find an existential reality that is considered alive through and through, and which involves a visible and an invisible part/sphere/world/land that are superimposed on the world of humanity. These existential spheres or "lands" seem to be all that the Egyptians were concerned about. This division seems to have pervaded their whole understanding of life, and therefore also their conceptual universe.

GENESIS—THE EGYPTIAN "BUBBLE" IN THE WATER

On a general level, Ancient Egypt resembled any other kinship-based society, past and present. In such societies, positions are linked to the reproductive conditions of the society, which is conditioned by its position in larger networks of exchange. This position, in turn, determines what kind of prestige economy is possible locally. The negotiation of these resources results in some form of prestige economy. Without a prestige economy, there would be no reason for social hierarchy, or any other kind of social differentiation.

Everything in this type of society are on personal relationships resulting in some kind of kinship system. As a result, someone must presumably have inaugurated the "system" to begin with, some founding fathers who were also the owner of the land and its resources. Therefore, social position is intimately connected to the individual's position in the kinship system and its genealogy. Locally it is important to understand who the first ancestors were and how they came into being. Genesis is a way to explain such issues. Stories of genesis are therefore also a means of depicting the present social order as primordial and everlasting.

Perplexingly, the ancestral world of Ancient Egypt was populated with all kinds of fantastic creatures. We see these creatures pictured everywhere on monuments and in papyri from Ancient Egypt. If one takes these images at face value, Egypt truly appears to be a land of wonder and magic.

Such wonders and marvels also appear to be reflected in Ancient Egyptian genesis stories. To many Western observers, these stories seem very exotic, almost incomprehensible, or even based on free fantasy. Their only purpose seems to be to offer some superficial explanation for the existence and order of the world, however bizarre. One might even surmise that they must have been invented for the sheer entertainment of the local populace.

However, Ancient Egypt was not a fantasy world, even though many might think so. The Ancient Egyptians' perceptions of the world and its "magical" inhabitants, as well as their "genesis stories" were not just free-floating fantasies only meant for public entertainment. Such symbolic expressions are always ways of attributing meaning to the surrounding world—notably its prestige economy—and as such, these symbolic structures must relate to the existing social organization, since meaning and social organization cannot be separated.

Even though most societies have stories about genesis (for instance, Adam and Eve, the Big Bang, etc.), there is no panhuman creation myth. The specific sequence and relationship between elements in these stories relate to the societies from which they originate, and to the specific forms of social organization in these societies. Therefore, "genesis stories" cannot be completely random.

We only have very flimsy references to "genesis" from early Egyptian history, or the conception of the beginning of the world. Later, however, we find very explicit references to how the Ancient Egyptians understood "genesis." These more comprehensive texts come from the "Pyramid Texts" located inside the pyramid of Unas from the fifth dynasty onward.

In the so-called Utterance 600, there is an explicit allusion to how the "cosmos" came about. Referring to the "work" of Atum (the primeval "god"), we read:

> You became high as the primeval mound; you arose as Benben in the House of the Phoenix in Heliopolis. You spat out as Shu, you coughed up as Tefnut, you placed your arms around them as the arms of *ka*, so that your *ka* might be in them. (See Faulkner 2007: 246); Mercer 2008: 363; this version from Assmann 2001: 119–20)

Since Heliopolis is mentioned in this text extract, this version of "genesis" has become known as the Heliopolis concept of creation (in contrast to other versions from Memphis and Thebes [David 2002: 81]). In this Utterance, we are informed about how Atum, "created" two children Shu (air) and Tefnut (fire). We also learn that Atum, by embracing his children, transferred his so-called *ka* to them.

Later in the same "Utterance," we are introduced to the rest of the primordial family. They are only referred to by name; no mention is made of who they are or what they are doing. This seems to be common knowledge and therefore not necessary to mention in the text.

Here, we read:

O Great Ennead who are in Heliopolis, Atum, Shu, Tefnut, Geb, Nut, Osiris, Isis Set, Nephthys, children of Atum—his heart is broad (glad) because of his children. (Mercer 2008: 364)

In this list of "gods," only the later child of Osiris and Isis, named Horus, is missing.

Nowhere do we find a complete "genesis" story in the written records (David 2002: 82). We only have references to what seems to be a corpus of (oral) narratives that was obviously common knowledge.

Many of these writings mention how the universe came into being (David 2002: 82). We find further fragments of the "genesis story" in Utterance 527 from the Pyramid Texts. Here, we read:

To say: Atum created by his masturbation in Heliopolis. He put his phallus in his fist, to excite desire thereby. The twins were born, Shu and Tefnut. (Mercer 2008: 296)

Tyldesley reconstruct the original oral genesis narrative from such fragments:

In the beginning nothing existed but the deep, dark water of Nun. There was no land and no sky. No gods, no people, no light and no time. Only the endless, motionless waters. But deep within the still waters of Nun there floated a perfect egg. And trapped within that perfect egg was a solitary spark of life. (2011: 37–38)

Tyldesley continues by explaining how, together, the twins Shu and Tefnut formed a void or "bubble in the water" of Nun. The birth and subsequent quarrel between the visible gods, Geb (earth) and Nut (sky), and the invisible gods, Shu and Tefnut caused "the bubble," or the world, as the Egyptians knew it, to come into being (2011: 51).

It is easy, then, to see these "gods" as representing aspects, or physical properties, of the "real" world—whatever that is. However, the category "real world" does not exist in the Egyptian worldview. For them, these properties were living organisms. The sun was not the sun; it was a person.

Atum did not create the world. He came into being. He was the origin of the cosmos. Everything else sprang from him (Assmann 2001: 120). Thereafter, the cosmos was fashioned in his image. As a being that came into existence by himself, he was both considered "the finished" and "the all," but also "the becoming one," designating the different aspects of his spontaneous act of coming into existence by himself (Assmann 2001: 120).

These two aspects were known by the Egyptians as Atum and Khepri/Kheprer, respectively: that is, "the all" and "the becoming." In this way, the two aspects of "coming into being" reflect the fundamental dichotomy in Ancient Egyptian cosmology and its categories. Atum expresses the *djet* aspect, that is, the lasting aspect of being that was mostly linked to the "gods"; and Khepri represents the *neheh* aspect of reality that was a more transient life form associated with the life of human beings.

The cosmos was made up of two categories, *djet* and *neheh*, and two complementary lands/"spheres." In accordance with this division of the cosmos, pre-genesis is described as a time when "there were not yet two things" (Goelet 2015: 152). Genesis thus "explains" the existential aspect of human existence. These basic aspects of being, *djet* and *neheh*, probably also serve as a prototype for the later "titles" of the pharaohs.

However, at this point in the "genesis" narrative, the story changes momentum, seemingly for no reason. A new breed of ancestors is introduced. The next generation of "gods" is different. Geb and Nut's children, Osiris, Isis, Set, and Nephthys are nothing like the rest of the family. At this point, the "story" takes a completely different turn. Or rather, it evokes a new existential dimension.

What came before in the primordial family cannot explain the characters of those who followed (Assmann 2001: 121). Suddenly, the "gods" become all too human. Strife and killing came into the world, and the "gods" now instigated conflicts and perpetrated killing. The good old days were over. It was a fall from grace. Still, the good old days were remembered in the texts as a time

[when] sky and earth had not yet come into being, before the human race came into being and deities were born, before death came into being.
Before that which was secure came into being, before strife came into being, before fear regarding the Eye of Horus came into being. (Assmann 2001: 122)

Now, even the "gods" seem to have become malignant. Set, murders Osiris, his brother. This much is clear from the Pyramid Text:

Isis comes, Nephtheys comes, one of them on the right, one of them on the left. One of them as a [screeching] bird, one of them (Nephthys) as a kite. They found Osiris, after his brother Set had felled him to the earth in Nedit. (All Pyramid Texts citations are taken from Mercer 2008, this part from Utterance 532.)

It is not clear if Set had an accomplice in his murder of Osiris, because we are also told:

Behold what Set and Thot have done, thy two brothers, who knew not to weep for thee. (Utterance 218)

Neither is it clear from these texts how Osiris died. Maybe he drowned:

Horus has counted the gods for thee, so that they cannot get away from thee, from the place where thou wast drowned. (Utterance 364)

Some terrible fate seems, however, to have befallen Osiris after his murder. His corpse appears to have been cut into pieces, completely dismembered. His sister had a big assembly job on her hands to make Osiris a complete human again:

Nephythes has assembled for thee all they limbs, in her name of . . . lady of builders. She has made them well for thee. (Utterance 364)

Horus seem to take part in Osiris's bodily reconstruction.

Horus has united for thee thy limbs and does not allow thee to be sick; he has put thee together, so that there is no disorder in thee. (Utterance 364 repeated in Utterance 367)

In the end, Osiris's sister succeeds in mending him:

Isis and Nephthys have healed thee, Horus is not far from thee, thou art his *ka*. (Utterance 364)

After having been reassembled, Osiris is now ready to travel with Re.

This is Horus who is in thine arms; he will avenge thee. It is pleasing to him to be again with thee, in thy name of "He of the horizon whence Re goes forth." (Utterance 368)

In no uncertain terms

the two doors of heaven are open for thee, that thou mayest go forth through them. (Utterance 374)

In more prosaic terms it is said that

the double doors of heaven are open for thee, the double doors of . . . are unfastened for thee; the double doors of the tomb are open for thee, the double doors of Nut are unfastened for thee. (Utterance 553)

Osiris is ready to leave.

Stand up Ladder of Set; stand up Ladder of Horus which was made for Osiris, that he may ascend upon it to heaven and do service of courtier to Re. (Utterance 478)

There is very little about the motive and execution of the murder. There are, however, some allusions to disapproval by the other "gods." After all, the murder caused some consternation, since it was the first of its kind. A completely new occurrence in the world.

It is also clear that the dead Osiris sired an heir. This seems not to be of great concern at this point in the narrative, which transpires in the depths of the pyramid. We simply learn that

it is Horus thy son, whom thou hast conceived; he has not put N (any dead pharaoh) over the dead. (Utterance 477)

There is nothing about how the dead man managed this feat, or with whom. This is all we are told in the Pyramid Text about the killing of Osiris, and the introduction of death. To progress in our understanding of the Ancient Egyptian thought system, we need the sordid details about what happened after the death of Osiris.

This information is only to be found in much later sources. It is not until the 18th Dynasty on the stela of Amenmose that we get a more comprehensive account of the fate of Osiris and his child (Tyldesley 2011: 104):

Raised the weary one's inertness, Received the seed, bore the heir, Raised the child in solitude, His abode unknown. (Tyldesley 2011: 104–5)

Together, the pyramid Utterances and the text from the stela leave little doubt: Set killed Osiris, cut him into pieces and threw the body parts in the Nile. After a prolonged search, Isis found the parts and reassembled them into a complete corpse. Or almost: we learn in a later text that Osiris' penis was missing. Isis "raised his inertness," had a child with the dead man, and gave birth to a son called Horus.

Plutarch later supplies all the details. However, his account, written in AD 120, leaves a great deal of room for "interpretation" (Tyldesley 2011: 107–9).

Plutarch also records that because of Osiris' dismemberment there are many so-called tombs of Osiris in Egypt (maybe reflected in the smaller pyramids found all over Egypt made by the same pharaoh). He also records that Isis held a funeral for each part when she found them, scattered throughout Egypt.

These thoughts are somewhat supported by the *Papyrus of Ani*, in which we read:

> As to *"that night of secreting of forms"*: it was when there was the burial of the forearm, the flanks, and the thighs of Osiris. (Faulkner and Goelet 2015: Plate14-A)

At this point, the focus of the narrative shifts towards Isis, Horus, and Set. Since the events inside the pyramid seems to be over, the "story" continues in "The Coffin Texts." Isis awakes, pregnant with the seed of her brother Osiris. The woman gets up quickly, her heart joyful because of the seed of her brother Osiris. She says, "O gods, I am Isis, the sister of Osiris, who mourns over the father of the gods; Osiris, who mediated the slaughter of the Two Lands, his seed is in my body. I have fashioned the form of a god in the egg as the son of him at the head of the Ennead, that he might assume rule over this land, the heir of his father Geb, who will put in a word on behalf of his father, who will kill Seth, the enemy of this father Osiris" (Assmann 2001: 130–1).

A second "genesis" is underway, this time performed by a dead man and his sister. We are on the threshold of a new division of the cosmos. So far, everything in the genesis narrative has transpired among "gods." Then Horus is born (Assmann 2001: 132).

However, with the birth of Horus, the cosmos had to change. Being born from a dead man, Horus was godlike but inherited his father's fate of being mortal. He was half god, half human. With the birth of Horus, the gods retired into an invisible realm, while the mortals lived among themselves in the Light world.

At this point, the "story" changes momentum again. Now, the "plot" turns to the relationship between Set and Horus, called *The contention between Set and Horus*. This part of the "story" has more in common with traditional drama. Here "the story" explores a political schism between seniority (Set) and ancestry (Horus).

Like in all dramas, this section of genesis starts by introducing a dilemma, or problem—in this case, who will inherit the throne, Set or Horus. Set has obviously already occupied the throne due to his seniority (never mind that he killed Osiris). Horus contests this because he is the legitimate heir (being the son of the "king" Osiris). After having introduced "the problem," a series of controversies follows in which these two characters engage each other in various disputes and struggles (probably to the great amusement of the listening "crowd," who knew the ending).

The whole charade ends with the inevitable: Horus is declared the rightful owner of the crown due to ancestry (Tyldesley 2011: 133–42). Everybody knew this is how it would end:

> Oh, Beautiful day! Sky and earth are in joy . . . Horus has arisen as ruler, the Ennead is in festival . . . the son of Isis, has arisen as ruler. . . . the son of Isis, has been assigned the office of his father, of Osiris.

At the same time, this story depicts an existential change in the cosmos. There is no doubt that the birth of Horus, and his enthronement, change the order of the cosmos. There are now two lands/realms of cosmos, and both of them rejoice.

> The entire double realm says to him (Horus): "beautiful is Horus on the throne of his father Amun-Re, the god who sent him out."

The character of these two realms is also clarified.

> Horus appears on the throne of Geb, the sky above his head, the earth under his feet. He took possession of the entire land; sky and earth were under his supervision [presumably "the two lands"]. Humankind were commended to him . . . what the sun encircles was subject to his will. (Assmann 2001: 142–7)

This division of the cosmos is further illustrated in "The Book of the Dead" (*Going Forth by Day*), in which we read:

> O all you gods of the soul-mansion who judge sky and earth in the balance, who give food and provision . . . [and to Re] May those who are above worship you, may those who are below worship you. (Faulkner and Goelet 2015: Plate 1-A)

Hence, the cosmos is divided into sky and earth, and above and below: the realm of gods and the realm of humans. May they both worship you, Re. Later we read:

> Hail to you, King of Kings, Lord of Lords, Ruler of Rulers, who took possession of the two lands [translator "probably means Upper and Lower Egypt"] even in the womb of Nut; he rules the plains of the Silent Lands [realm of the dead], even he the golden of body, blue of head, on whose arms is turquoise. . . . May you grant power in the sky, might of earth, and vindication in the God's Domain. (Faulkner and Goelet 2015: Plate 2-B)

In this extract, it seems that we are informed about the correct meaning of "The Two Lands," as "power in the sky; might on earth." This is corroborated by the reference to the fact that the Ruler took possession of the two lands in the womb of Nut (there is nothing geo-political going on here). After the birth of Horus, these are the two realms of the cosmos.

Horus is now the lawful "king" of the Light-land and the Netherworld, the two realms that the sun encircles. The cosmos has changed and death has been introduced. It is still possible that "he who recites this spell [*sic*] will be alive in the realm of the dead" (Assmann 2001: 115). Death is obviously not the end of the road.

In the last part of the narrative, the initial inheritance problem between Set and Horus is resolved according to social conventions. Order is restored. Everybody can relax. Now the genesis story is complete.

It is clear that Ancient Egyptian genesis is based on a "family" comprising successive generations. First, we have self-creation and self-impregnation. From a deep watery nothing, Atum came into being all by himself. His name means "to be nothing" and "to be everything." Since he was alone, Atum masturbated to create his children, Shu (meaning "emptiness" or "void" and Tefnut (tef translates as "spit," and may have been associated with some type of moisture, such as morning dew) (Tyldesley 2011: 45, Pingh 2002: 196).

Having given birth to these "children," Atum embraced them to transfer his *ka* to them (Pingh 2002: 64). After a series of events, Shu and Tefnut separate from their father and perform the cosmos' first sexual union, after which Tefnut gave birth to another pair of deities, a son Geb (earth) and a daughter Nut (sky). However, they clung so passionately together that nothing could slip between them (Pingh 2002: 65).

Shu had to step in and solve the crisis. He had to create a space between Geb and Nut where their children could live. This space also made it possible for the sun to rise for the first time and drive away the primeval darkness. Shu is often pictured as standing with his arms raised to support the arched body of Nut; "raised arms" also being the hieroglyph for *ka* (Pingh 2002: 65). This is how the cosmos became fixed with an upper sky (Nut), the earth (Geb), and with air (Shu) in between, all encircled by the dark primeval water of Nun.

The separation of Geb and Nut made it possible for their children to be born. For some reason, the latter had completely different statuses. In descending birth order these were: Osiris, Isis, Set and Nephthys. Now the cosmos was complete, and its creator could dream up all kinds of beings to populate his new world. All manner of animals, fish and reptiles, in addition to humanity.

Then Osiris was killed by Set, but nonetheless managed to have a postmortem child with Isis, named Horus. The Ancient cosmological genealogy thus looks like this:

```
                        Atum
                         |
        ┌────────────────────────────────┐
        |                                |
       Shu             Tefnut
                         |
        ┌────────────────────────────────┐
        |                                |
       Geb               Nut
                         |
  ┌──────────┬──────────────────┬──────────────┐
  |          |                  |              |
Osiris     Isis             Nephthys         Set
           |
         Horus
```

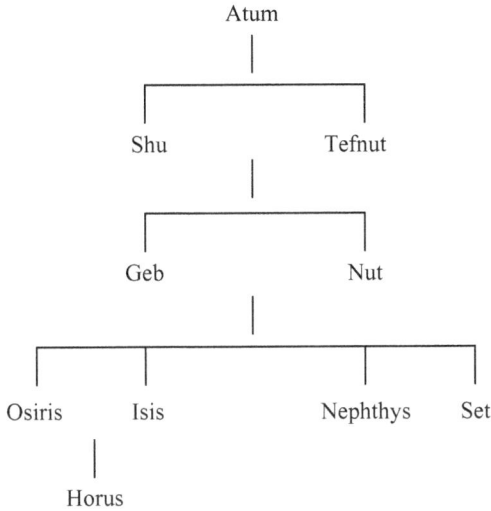

Note that it is not the narrative and all its sordid details that are important. Rather, what is significant are the elements in the narrative and the order in which they occur. One might speculate endlessly—as indeed many have done—about how to interpret all the events and happenings in these ancient stories. The events are entertaining, to say the least, but it is the cosmological message that such stories convey that is important. What is significant is the way in which the elements (persons) order (explain) social reality. Otherwise, we would just drown in details.

Therefore, the real importance of such stories lies in the way they establish the rightful relations between social categories, the order of things, and relationships between people. Accordingly, I posit that this ongoing "story" introduces us to the fundamental categories of Ancient Egyptian cosmology and their conceptual order.

There are two ways to read such genesis narratives. One is cosmological, the other political, and the two presuppose each other. On the cosmological level, we observe that Atum "comes into being" by his own effort, so to speak, out of nowhere, or as the Ancients would have it, out of a deep still, watery darkness. A big, watery "big bang."

Atum came into being by creating a bubble in the water. His children populated this space. Because he "became" all by himself, Atum had two inherent qualities, as his name also implies: "To be nothing" and "to be everything." In other words, to use Ancient Egyptian vocabulary, he encompassed the two qualities of life: the basic Egyptian categories, *djet* and *neheh*, the "permanence" and "transient" nature of being that seems to have pervaded all of Ancient Egyptian "reality."

He then embraced his children, thereby transferring his *ka* to them. He also transferred the two qualities that he possessed to his children, so that each came to stand for one of the aspects/categories/properties of social "reality": "Shu is Eternal Recurrence and Tefnut is Eternal Sameness" (Pingh 2002: 65), *neheh* and *djet*. In this case as moisture that comes and goes and emptiness, that is permanent, respectively. Then came Nut (sky) and Geb (earth), who seem to be yet another extension of this division of reality.

"Genesis" was complete. Now "the cosmos" consisted of the elements that the Ancients deemed necessary. A fully functional world was now in place. It was encircled by water that made it possible for Re to travel around the world in his boat, being visible during daytime and disappearing into Nun at night.

But something was missing! So far, Atum had created eternal life for himself and his children. Although they could, of course, live in some corner of the cosmos, there was no space for mortal humans. Death had to be introduced somehow. At some point, there had to be another creation, one that made the world of humans possible. This is also where the "persons" of the "genesis" narrative change character.

It seems that the last generation with Osiris, Isis, Set and Nephthys had to be different from their parents' generation in order to prepare for the cosmos to be divided into "two lands." Humans would thereafter live in their own domain separate from that of the "gods."

This last generation became very human-like. They argued, they fought, and to cap it all, Set killed his own brother, Osiris. Death was thus introduced, and with it a new division of the cosmos that introduced a new distinction between everlasting and transient beings. This time, the distinction was between "gods" and humans, who now related to one another as *djet* and *neheh*, respectively—the major categories of Ancient thought.

Osiris was killed and dismembered by his brother. Isis managed to put the pieces together again, except for the penis, which had been eaten by a fish. She then made a fake penis contraption by which she managed to become pregnant and give birth to Horus. So humankind was "created" by a fake penis. Things could only go downhill from there. In this light, it is not surprising that humans are doomed to die. Theirs are not eternal lives. This everlasting dimension of the cosmos was removed to a separate sphere for the ancestors only.

Osiris and his missing penis performed, so to speak, a negating or inverse "creation" compared to that undertaken by Atum when he created the cosmos. A real penis created "Gods," humans was created by a fake one. Atum brought everlasting life into being through masturbation; Osiris created short-lived human lives with a fake penis. By dying, Osiris entered into, or created, a separate kind of existence—in an existential realm that humans could only reach by dying (Pingh 2002: 83).

Osiris's "becoming"/"creation" had to be inverted in order to produce a division between the realms of the "gods" and humanity. The *djet—neheh* aspect of reality was initially a horizontal relationship between (equals) "gods." With the murder of Osiris, this also changed into a vertical and hierarchical relationship between gods and humans.

Suddenly, the cosmos had two realms and four categories. Ancient life therefore consisted of four basic properties:

Invisible realm (gods):	*djet*	-	*neheh*	eternal life
Visible realm (humans)	*neheh*	-	*djet*	passing life

The logical consequence is that everything had a *djet* and a *neheh* aspect both in the visible and in the invisible realm. But with the separation of the cosmos into two realms, these aspects also had their counter parts in the other realm. Therefore, these realms were interconnected, so that a *neheh* in the visible realm had to have a *djet* both in the visible and invisible realm, likewise with a *djet*. So everything was connected in long lines of interaction, creating a world that was alive through and through.

Up until this point, there is nothing extraordinary about Ancient cosmology. It pretty much follows other kinship-based societies inasmuch as it had a realm for ancestors and one for living humans, with the two somehow interconnected.

Still, we immediately notice that the Ancient Egyptian genesis story was cast in the form of a genealogy. This brings us to the political content of the narrative. Casting the story in genealogical terms is not strictly necessary, and is certainly not a universal way of accounting for genesis.

Anyway, the existential part of existence has to be given some sort of direction. Existentialism is not free floating. It will not lend support to just any kind of social system. It has to be "written" into genesis. Ancient Egyptian divine genealogy is particular in this respect. It starts and ends with one person: Atum at the beginning, and Horus at the end. Nothing more was needed. In a relatively short version of the genealogy, we are introduced to the "king" of Egypt and his divine origin. The political aspects of genesis do not need further personages.

We also need to account for the last part of the genesis narrative, *The contention between Set and Horus*. We immediately notice that this is no typical, universal model for a conflict over who gets to rule. That this could ever have become a problem was due to the way in which the Ancient Egyptian kinship system related uncles to brothers' sons. In most kinship systems, these two characters never come into contact with one another, and there will never be a dispute about who of them will inherit the throne. Never ever.

This inheritance issue can only arise in a kinship system based on a *matrilateral x-cousin system with avuncular residence*. This is the only kind of kinship system which brings "uncle and brother's son" into close contact with each other. In this system, "the uncle" has the local authority, based on his seniority, while "the son" is the heir to the throne, by birthright. The problem arises because the brother's son lives at his uncle's place. This problem cannot have escaped the notice of the ancient Egyptians. At any rate, they told long stories about the inherent schism in their kinship system. In such systems, the brother of the present "ruler" marries into a local group into which the "ruler's" son also marries. This produces the conundrum of inheritance.

Finally, but importantly, we have the problem of the "mound" (or how this word should be translated). Having established that the social system was expressed through kinship, and that the genesis narrative establishes a relationship between the "king" and the original "becoming," we are also introduced to a primordial "mound" that rises from the undifferentiated water.

The following section is conjecture on my part. Nonetheless, the "mound" gives cause for concern. There are many indications in the Ancient texts that "mound" should be understood as "mountain," and that this is connected to gold prospecting.

Still, for many Egyptologists, the simplest explanation of this "mound" is that it must resemble the Nile Valley after inundation. As the water recedes, patches of land begin to appear. This would be a fitting explanation if Egypt had always been an agricultural society.

However, this is not the case. Looking at the historical record, the standard Egyptological interpretation of "the mound" as an agricultural phenomenon does not seem to make sense. We should remember that Egypt was not an agricultural land until very late in its history. Social hierarchy in Upper Egypt started long before Egypt became an agricultural society. In the beginning, at the time of Badarian and Naqada, the Ancients were herders and hunters in the Eastern Desert, and their leaders always defined themselves in relation to gold.

Prestige and position must have been connected to this situation. Initially, the elite did not identify with agriculture but with gold. Isis even called her child "Horus of Gold" Status and gods were all about gold from the mountains. After having brought his heart down from the mountain, Re was reassembled as a golden falcon:

> They give me worship when I appear, having being reassembled as a fair falcon of gold upon the pointed stone. Re comes in daily to give judgment, and I sit among those elder gods of the Lower sky [the sky in the Netherworld]. (Faulkner and Goelet 2015: Plate 25-A, B)

In another extract, we clearly see that Re is identified with gold:

I worship you when you set in the Primordial water, and I set you in my heart which is not inert, O you who are more divine than the gods. Praise to you who rise in gold and who illuminate the Two Lands by day at your birth! (Faulkner and Goelet 2015: Plate 21-A)

Here there is a strong connection between Re's journey from the Primordial water into day, where he appears "in gold." In another instance, he illuminates the "Two Lands" (which should read "the two realms of existence").

Turn your face to the West that you may illuminate the Two Lands (*sic*) with fine gold. (Faulkner and Goelet 2015: Plate 19-B)

"Gods" and gold seem almost interchangeable in these examples.

Furthermore, the Wadis leading into the Nile valley are also where, from an early date, we find petroglyphs with boats and people with their hands raised in what that look like *ka*-gestures. A gesture that appears to be part of some kind of worship, which would be befitting since all the wealth of the Egypt came from this area. These motives recur in the so-called "painted tomb," the "grave" of a nobleman, which was probably connected to the gold deposits in the desert.

Maybe the "mound" was, in fact, a mountain in the eastern desert, which would, prestige-wise, make much more sense that an agricultural land appearing out of water in a place where nobody lived at the dawn of Egypt's history.

Furthermore, we read:

Awake in peace, may you awake peacefully; Horus of Behdet awakes in peace. The gods awake early to adore your *ba*. O exalted winged beetle who ascends to the sky! It is he who "opens the sphere" in the sky goddess, and fills the earth with gold dust, who comes to life in the eastern mountains, who sleeps daily in Behdet. (Assmann 2001: 38)

Gold, Horus and the eastern mountains are obviously connected. In "The Book of the Dead" (*Going Forth by Day*), there are also references to a mountain:

Your rise and shine on the back of your mother (the sky), having appeared in glory as King of the gods. Your mother Nut shall use her arms on your behalf in making greetings. The Manu-mountain receives you in peace, Maat embraces you at all seasons. (Faulkner and Goelet 2015: Plate 1-A)

Mountains and Maat (cosmic order) are obviously also connected phenomena.

In the *Papyrus of Ani* we are introduced to the notion of a hill:

What does it mean? It means Re when he began to rule what he made, when he began to appear as king, before the Supports of Shu had come into being, when he was upon the hill which is in Hermopolis, when he destroyed the Children of Impotence on the hill which is in Hermopolis. (Faulkner and Goelet 2015: plate 7-A)

In this extract, there is a clear link between primordial times and a hill. When Re created himself, and became "king" (before Shu came into being), he was upon a *hill*. It also seems that Re begins his diurnal travels from a mountain:

I have gone up from the coffer into the Night-bark, I have brought my heart from the eastern mountains, I have alighted in the Day-bark, there are brought to me those of ancient times bowing down, and they give me worship when I appear. (Faulkner and Goelet 2015: Plate 25-A)

Re's travel obviously takes him and his heart through a mountain. Maybe it is the primordial mound—a mountain of gold. Perhaps, more plausibly, it is a prototype of the pyramids.

Mountains and other topographical features in the landscape had a special role. One such thing was the Qorn in the western cliffs at Thebes; another was the aket (concave shaped) declivity. These two places probably achieved their statuses because of their shape, the Qorn resembling a pyramid (maybe there was a "natural" prototype for this kind of construction after all) the other serving as an image of the birthplace of the sun (Lloyd 2014: 230).

Also other locations in the mountains had special value, as Lloyd call sacred spaces. Quarries and mines in such areas as Sinai, Gebel es-Silsila, Aswan and the Wadi Hammamat, links the "gods" closely to the gold prospecting. Places here were called "august" and "primeval" (Lloyd 2014: 231). Finally, Wadi Hammamat was "the god's palace," and the mountain termed *ta netjer*, "Gods Land'". There seem to be a straight line from the primeval time to "gods," gold and the pharaohs.

It was such a potent place thought to be enlivened by the "gods":

Thus, the greywacke stone cut from cliffs in the Wadi Hammamat was regarded as having life-giving powers that made I ideal for use as a sarcophagus for a king whose corpse could assimilate divinizing power from it, and the same held true of gold, the colour and substance of the god's flesh, which could function in the same way when used for masks or coffins. (Lloyd 2014: 231)

Pharaohs were always the masters of gold. It was the only explanation for their social position. Grain cannot create such steep hierarchies. Pharaohs even had a so-called gold title in the form of a Falcon (Horus) on top of the hieroglyph for gold, and furthermore "gods" had skins of gold. As Re said, "my skin is of pure gold" (Frankfort 1978 [1948]: 46). Had there been no gold, there would have been no pharaohs, and the ancestral world would have been organized differently.

What we can say is that the reproductive conditions in Egypt, with its prestige economy based on the exchange of gold for foreign goods, were a key issue in the workings of the social system. This, in turn, influenced the character of Egyptian cosmology and the way the Ancients "organized" their "gods." Without gold, Ancient Egypt would have had a different kinship system and there would have been no reason for a dispute between Set and Horus over who was the rightful heir to the throne.

Altogether, we have seen that Ancient cosmology and its notion of genesis were politically organized. While the idea of a double realm—two lands with one section for the ancestors and one for the living—is common to kinship-based societies, it does not follow logically that these spheres should be connected through a strict hierarchical genealogy. As a result, the Egyptian genealogical interpretation of "genesis" means that the incumbent "king" in Ancient Egypt was always directly related to the origin of life. This is a political interpretation. The pharaoh was, in this light, the human representative of the cosmic principles created by Atum. This was an existential world and a political world. This was ancient Egyptian cosmology.

Chapter 4

Ancient Egyptian Concept of Personhood

Living in Two Lands

Ancient Egyptians negotiated their reproductive conditions that were highly related to their external relationships. This in turn created conditions in the social fabric that the local population had to make sense of giving a special Egyptian culture, with a notion about the constitution of a double-sided "cosmos," its creation, the role of human in this and how they managed to live in two realms of existence.

Because of these negotiations, Ancient Egyptian cosmology divided the "cosmos" into two realms/lands. Ancient Egyptian notions of "genesis" explore how this cosmos came into existence and why it consisted of two lands, one for "gods" and one for living humans. Ancient concept of personhood formed part of this cosmology. Living in a dual cosmos influences how people conceive of themselves as human beings. Egyptian personhood revolved around how the living related to the land of the "gods" and ancestors. Existence became a matter of life and death.

"Genesis" presents Osiris, Isis, Set and Horus as the instigators of the division of the cosmos into two realms/lands. Horus, who was born of a dead man, was considered neither fully divine nor fully human. His status made him different from his subjects and allowed him to speak directly with the gods (Tyldesley 2011: 230).

According to Frankfort, this capacity was expressed through widespread reference to the "king," which indicated that a "god" was embodied in the physical frame of the pharaoh. This term is ordinarily translated as "His Majesty," but its original meaning is "body," (*hm*) and "physical appearance" (Frankfort 1978 [1948]: 45).

This term is therefore a reference to the outward appearance of the "king," who was thought to embody "the Lord of All." References to the ruling pharaoh of any given period should then read "during the Incarnation of

'King N,'" or "during the lifetime of the Embodiment of 'King N.'" Meaning that "King N," who mortals knew and saw, was a particular incarnation or embodiment of the "god"—not a mere mortal individual like everybody else. Just a different looking incarnation of the same person (his body was as such disposable, a transient "housing"). So, Horus was always the same "person"; he just looked different from one generation to the next (Frankfort 1978 [1948]: 45).

All these turns of phrase suggest that earthly rulers incorporated an immortal "god" (Frankfort 1978 [1948]: 45). Horus was, therefore, part of both realms of existence, and this idea is vividly illustrated on temple walls, where he is shown in perpetual interaction with other "gods" (Pingh 2002: 85). This status separated the "king" from his subjects and made it possible for him to speak directly to the "gods" (Tyldesley 2011: 230). He so to speak, lived among then in the invisible realm of existence.

Other people than the pharaoh had the ability to pass between the worlds of the living and the dead (Pingh 2002: 85). The So-called priests (for lack of a better translation) had the power to communicate directly with the invisible beings in the land of the ancestors. Some of these "priests" were even reported to have had the power to enter the *Duat* (Netherworld) while still alive. That, however, was a risky business, and the Egyptian literature is full of warnings against the misuse of such powers (Pingh 2002: 84).

This conceptualization of the "king" and the "priests" (and their powers) could not stand alone. The relationship of these two types of actor to the Netherworld had to rely on a more general principle common to all people, but played out in a particular way by these specific actors.

This common principle found its expression in the belief that "gods" also communicated with ordinary people through temples, oracles, and in dreams. Dead people were an active force in the life of the living. Ordinary mortals were not able to enter the *Duat* directly, but everybody nonetheless communicated with the dead.

One way in which ordinary people communicated with the dead was by writing letters to the deceased. In those letters, many asked the dead to intervene in their daily affairs, to help with problems, or to solve domestic disputes.

Such "letters" (also known from the anthropological literature) show the intimacy that existed between the living and the dead in Ancient Egypt.

> How are you in the West [the land of the dead] taking care of you as you desire?
> . . . I did not [garbled] a [funerary spell] in your presence when I perpetuated your name upon earth. Remove the infirmity of my body! Please become a spirit [*akh* ?] for me [before] my eyes so that I might see you in a dream fighting on my behalf.

And,

To the able spirit [*akh*] Ankhiry: What have I done against you wrongfully for you to get into this evil disposition in which you are? What have I done against you? As for what you have done, it is your laying hands upon me though I committed no wrong against you. From the time that I was living with you as a husband until today, what have I done against you that I should have to conceal it?

And,

Moreover let a healthy son be born to me for you are an able spirit [*akh*]. Now as for those two maidservants . . . who have caused Seny to be afflicted, confound them! And banish for me whatever afflictions are directed against my wife, whom you know I have need of. Banish them completely!

And,

What about the maidservant Imiu who is ill? Aren't you [the deceased] fighting on her behalf day and night, with whoever, male or female, is acting against her? . . . Fight on her behalf anew this day that her household may be maintained and water poured out for you [as a funerary offering]. (Teeter 2011: 155–7)

In these excerpts, sickness and disease are a person's downfall, and it is all the fault of an ancestor. In this way, the dead greatly influenced the "land" of the living. It seems that the dead had the power both to inflict sicknesses and harm on people. But they were also capable of acting as benevolent beings who could ease problems. One had better stay on good terms with the dead. Offerings were advisable.

Dreams were another way in which ordinary people communicated with the dead (an ability widely known in anthropology). In dreams, the dead could reveal themselves to the living. The term for dream, *rewt*, is also derived from the word for "awake" (Teeter 2011: 158). Its literal meaning is "to come awake" (Asaad 2015: 13), reflecting that the dreamer was awake in another part of the realm of existence. In hieroglyphics, a dream is expressed by the symbol of a bed, combined with the symbol of an open eye. It reads "awaken within sleep" (Asaad 2015: 13).

From later dream books, we learn that in dreams people could see the "spirits" of the dead. Dreams also made it possible for people to join their own dead family members. Some letters written to the dead mention a community of the deceased in a place called "one city." Here, we read, "you have witnesses with you in the one city" (Teeter 2011: 158). This suggests that the dead live together in "one city" (such stories also occur in the ethnographic records).

Not everyone was happy about his/her experiences while traveling in the invisible land of existence during sleep. One man found it necessary to write a letter to his dead father complaining that he was being bothered by their servant, Seni, who had died sometime before:

> Indeed, let his lord take heed so that he [Seni] no longer creates disturbances. He should be guarded until he has ceased to visit me . . . once and for all. (Teeter 2011: 158–9)

Sleep was intimately connected with the part of the person called the *ba*. In hieroglyphics, the *ba* was depicted as a human-headed bird hovering above a sleeping body (Asaad 2015: 13). It was therefore the adventures of the *ba* that were experienced during sleep. While the *ba* was away, the body would be inert: it slept (in many ethnographic places considered "a small dead").

These observations indicate that the *ba* left the sleeping body to roam around in the invisible realm of ancestors and "gods." Consequently, everybody lived in two realms of existence. Every living person had a body in the visible realm, and a *ba* that traveled in the land of the dead when the person fell asleep. Seen from this perspective, ancestors were an existential reality. Everybody could encounter them.

Sleep and death seem to have been regarded as similar phenomena. This is evident on a funerary stela (from a later period; however, this conception of life and death is unlikely to have changed):

> The west [the land of the dead] it is the land of sleep. Darkness weighs on the dwelling-place. Those who are there sleep in their mummy-forms. (Tyldesley 2011: 166)

In both "modes" of being, the person was thought to be in a different state than the ordinary state of wakefulness. A part of them was, in these moments, living in the invisible land of the ancestors (a phenomenon also well-known in the ethnographic material).

Not only were sleep and death regarded as similar phenomena; the way these phenomena were depicted was also very similar. At death, the *ba* is shown as a bird hovering over a corpse instead of an eye or *ba* hovering over a sleeping person. The *ba* is also shown flying down the tomb shaft to rejoin the corpse. We have a papyrus from later times saying, "May his Ba not separate itself from his corpse forever." In tombs, the dead are depicted as birds with human heads, sometimes supplied with arms, and the dead could come to earth and flutter under the rays of the sun in the form of birds (Frankfort 2000 [1948]: 97–98):

Thou shalt come in and go out, thy heart rejoicing in the favor of the Lord of the Gods, a good burial [being thine] after a venerable old age, when age has come, thou assuming thy place in the coffin, and joining earth on the high ground of the west. Thou shalt change into a living Ba, and surely he will have power to obtain bread and water and air and thou shalt take shape as a heron or swallow, as a falcon or a bittern, whichever thou pleases. . . . . Thy Ba shall not depart from thy corpse and thy Ba shall become divine with the blessed dead. . . . Thou shalt go up to the sky, and shalt penetrate the Netherworld in all forms that thou likest. (Frankfort 1975 [1948]: 98–99)

Here, we have yet another expression of the principle of a *ba*-bird hovering above a corpse or a sleeping person. We have already met this constellation. It is also one of the earliest symbolic expressions of such a relationship. It finds its most vivid expression in the *serekh*, the emblem of the early "kings." In this emblem, we find exactly the same imagery as in the images depicting sleep and death. The *serekh* image consists of a *ba*-bird in the form of a falcon hovering above, or sitting on, a grave (enclosure), making the same kind of connection between the two lands as the "signs" for dreams and the dead.

Therefore, the *serekh* expresses the same cosmic principle as the understanding of dreams and death. In the *serekh* instance, the "king" couples together a grave and a *ba*-bird in a kind of "trademark," which portrays him as intimately connected to the land of the "gods." Horus/the falcon hovering over a grave gives the impression that he is the envoy of the "gods." He is, in fact, the *ba* of some ancestor in the invisible land.

At the time that the *serekh* was introduced, we do not know for whom the *ba*-falcon was flying, that is, who was in the grave (later, it was Osiris. I will return to this issue). Yet what this shows is that this was a very ancient way of understanding the "cosmos." Furthermore, it becomes a moot point to call this the pharaoh's "Falcon name," as the falcon only represents half the constellation. It rather represent a depiction of "he who was able to live in the two lands."

Of course, the same double cosmic constellation is repeated in all the other pharaoh "titles." Most of these are hard to interpret and translate, since we do not know the etymologies of the creatures involved. It is, however, especially clear in the pharaoh's so-called "gold title." Here, once again, we see the *ba*-falcon hovering, this time over the sign for gold. Since we know that gold was considered the skin of the "gods," this "title" conjures up the same image of the pharaoh as one who lives between the land of the "gods" and the land of human beings. It identified the pharaoh with Re who was assembled as a golden Falcon. Maybe the Ancient meant that it was the pharaohs Re incarnation.

It is now clear that the common principle for Horus's constitution and the lives of the common people was integrated in the notion of the *ba*. It kept a person awake (or conscious) in both "lands," and made it possible for common people to travel among the ancestors while they were sleeping. However, upon death, the relationship between the two lands, and between the "body" and the *ba*, was reversed.

In this situation, the *ba* kept the corpse alive at night in the Netherworld. During the daytime, the *ba* fluttered around like a bird in the visible land. That is why "The Book of the Dead" is called *Going Forth by Day* in Egyptian. This is exactly what the *ba*-bird does. It goes forth by day.

Significantly, Frankfort translates the term, *ba* as "animated"—which has nothing to do with the conventional way of translating *ba* as "a soul"—it can, moreover, mean "manifestation" of "the animated" (1978 [1948]: 64), that is, the conscious moving body. So a *ba* enlivens the body, dead or alive (this could also be the reason that pyramid are called Appearances and are associated with the "kings" *ba*).

This common principle expressed by the *ba* extends to the "gods" in general. For mortals to be able to communicate with the "gods," the former had to provide them with a place to stay when they entered the land of the living. Such places are what are now called temples. To the Ancients, these constructions were just resting places for their "gods." In these places, there was a room called *djesr djesru*, which translates as "the bedroom of the god." In this room, there was a replica of the "god" in the form of a statue (Teeter 2011: 41).

These statues were mostly made of precious metal. There is, for instance, a statue of Horus seated on a throne, forty-two centimeters tall. It is cast in silver (representing the "god's" bones), overlaid with a gold "skin," and it has rock crystal eyes.

Such "statues"— actually abode for the "gods" to rest in—were placed all over Egypt. In themselves, the statues were not "gods." They merely served as a transient receptacle for the presence of the "god's" *ba*. These statues provided a physical form (*ka*) in which the *ba* of the "god" could reside, so that human beings could communicate with their "god" (Teeter 2011: 43–44).

It seems that the *ba* of "gods" dwelled in "heaven," because there are references to *ba*'s that "come[s] from heaven [to see] its monuments." There is also a reference to the *ba* of Osiris

flying out of the heavens like a hawk with glittering plumage. He soars like a falcon to his [shrine] at Dendera. He beholds his sanctuary. Then he sees his secret aspect [the statue] and installs himself upon his image [*sekhem*]. (Teeter 2011: 44).

As Teeter concludes from such text extracts

once filled with and enlivened by the *ba* of the god, the cult statue becomes the *ka*, or physical form of the god. (Teteer 2011: 44)

"God" rests in his/her shrine after the *ba* has united with the image/receptacle that is its *ka*. There was, however, no explicit way in which the "gods" could be summoned to their statues. Building these houses seems to have been enough (Teteer 2011: 44).

It seems that a *ba* needed a *ka*; they even seem to have needed two "bodies." When Osiris's *ba* descended from the heavens to take up (other *ka*) life in his "statues"/*ka*, his corpse would still be lying firmly buried in the pyramid. So the *ba* would travel from his corpse in the invisible land to his *ka* in the visible land. He had a body/*ka* in both lands. The same principle applies to a dead person, who is a "corpse" at night and a fluttering *ba*-bird during the daytime, with the *ba* residing in the "corpse" at night and in a bird in the daytime. *Ba's* were apparently not able to just float around; they needed an abode, some form of "body"/*ka* such as a corpse, statue, bird, and so on. *Ba's* enlivened these "bodies."

In this way, it seems that everybody needed a double, a *ka* (Wenke 2009: 268) to live "a full life" in the two realms of existence. So the notion of *ka* was another principle that was common to "gods," "kings," and humans. The "god" Khnum was thought to manufacture a *ka* for everyone, at the same time as he manufactured actual living people from clay on his potter's wheel.

While the "gods" had a *ka* in the visible land for their *ba*'s to rest in, living humans had a body in the visible world and an equivalent "body" in the invisible world, which was called a *ka*. "The outside living body," *ht*, was regarded as an essential part of people and their personalities (Lloyd 2014: 211)—it was the place where the *ba* resided during daytime, enlightening the person and making s/he conscious.

Horus was, once again, a special case. He is, of course, the only one to have his *ka* portrayed on monuments (since these places only referred to the royals). Frankfort informs us that the "king's" *ka* is born together with the king as his twin, and that the twin accompanies Horus through life. Although presumably nobody expected to actually meet this royal twin walking around in broad daylight, it nonetheless formed part of his/her person. However, ordinary people might have met the king's "twin"—or somebody else's—in their dreams.

Unlike the common people, the "king" therefore lived simultaneously in both realms of existence. As a living ancestor, he could travel freely between his two different "bodies." Horus's body could therefore not just perish, since he had two bodies that enjoyed an equal footing. His visible body was forever renewable as the Embodiment of his body in the invisible world, as a "god." The pharaoh was therefore an eternal Horus. Horus' "body" had to be a continuous representation of the same "person," that is, the same substance.

Taken together, Horus's position rested on a belief in the general continuation of everybody's *ba*, and that everybody had a *ka*. If people just died and disappeared off the face of the earth, Horus could not have had an eternal life (even in different bodies). For Horus to continue to be *the* sole ruler there had to be a principle of continuity that everybody experienced, and this principle rested on the premise that everyone had a *ba* and a *ka*, and that people's *ba* made excursions into the invisible realm when they fell asleep.

Let me sum up. We have now assembled all aspects of the common principle that united the people of Ancient Egypt—from "gods," to "kings" to commoners—as well as insight into their different modes of being. This principle constituted the local interpretation, or negotiation, of how people could live in two lands. We now know the entire repertoire of forms that could exist between a body/corpse and its *ba*:

Invisible land	Visible land
Sleep	Body/ba
Gods	Ka/statue
Corpse	Ba/bird
"King"	Ka/Ba

We can now see that the Ancient Egyptians had four different forms of interaction between the two lands of existence, that is, between the land of the "gods"/ancestors and the land of the living. This is the cultural logic of Ancient Egyptian personhood, based on their cosmological schema of living in two lands. Everybody's mode of existence followed the same basic logic.

As is evident in the above diagram, the mode of being plays out differently for "gods," "kings," and humans. Humans go to sleep and encounter the "gods" in their dreams. The "gods" live in the invisible realm, but have to make themselves noticed in the realm of the living by having their *ba*'s dwell in some form of receptacle, for example, in statues made for that very purpose. This enabled humans and "gods" to communicate.

"Dead" people had a similar problem to the "gods," but they had no sanctuaries or statues in which to dwell, so they had to fly around in the form of birds when they left the invisible land they had been confined to, so that they could see what was going on among their living relatives.

In contrast to "gods" and humans in general, Horus, the living-dead god, had to live in both lands/realms simultaneously to verify his godly status while existing as a dead/living human. His *ba* could therefore presumably travel freely between the two realms of existence, since it had a "body" in the world of humans and a *ka* in the ancestral land.

Burial practices reflect the Egyptian concept of personhood as consisting of *ba*'s and *ka*'s. The practice of mummification and the handling of the corpse clearly shows that it was treated within such a division of personhood, in which different body parts represented the *ba* and the *ka*. Herodotus gives us one of the most comprehensive accounts of the mummification process; otherwise, the material is rather meager.

According to him, the process began with washing the body. Then, an incision was made in the left side of the abdomen to allow for the removal of the major organs (Teeter 2011: 135). During mummification, the lungs, liver, stomach, and intestines were removed, preserved and placed in a canopic jar that was placed alongside the corpse. Not every internal organ was removed from the corpse, however. The heart was left in place.

This very particular treatment of the internal organs clearly shows that this procedure had no practical function. To remove some of the internal organs was not a solution to prevent imminent rotting or fast decay. Such thinking merely reflects Western concerns about decaying corpses. All the organs would pose the same problem, so if rotting were the major concern in the mummification process, the heart would have had to be removed too.

Instead, the mummification-process followed a cultural logic that was based on the Ancient understanding of personhood. The heart was considered the center of intelligence and it would therefore also logically be the place where the Ancients believed that consciousness/"animation" of the "body" was located. The heart would have been the organ from where the *ba* enlivened the body.

Moreover, since the heart was the center of a person's accomplishments and his/her virtues in life, it could not be removed from the corpse. The heart was the seat of a person's actions, according to local lore it would also have to face judgment before a tribunal of "gods" before entering the invisible realm of the other ancestors (Tyldesley 2010: 164). If it was heavier than a feather, the person would suffer eternal damnation. The heart had to follow the corpse.

By contrast, the intestines had another destiny in the embalming process. They had to be taken out. They were probably looked at as another inner body, a *ka* that had to be taken out of the corpse and placed on its own. Ethnographically we know that the intestines are often seen as a second skin, or an inner body on its own. The heart would then represent the *ba*, and the intestines the *ka* (the same "categories" must inform all aspects of social life, or something would be amiss).

In this way, all Ancient Egyptian people had double identities. They had a "body" that lived among the living, and they had a "body" that lived among the dead. They had two parts to their personhood, which lived relatively separate lives. As we know from ethnography, such parallel worlds can exist on equal terms in kinship-based societies.

We still need to know how all these elements of personhood interacted, and how the elements related to one other. We now know that while the living person was awake, his *ba* would reside in his heart; while when s/he was asleep the *ba* lived in the land of the ancestors enliven the *ka* of that person who would then be traveling around in the invisible world. Logic dictates that when the human body was awake, the *ba* was with the person, at this time its *ka* must have been asleep, and therefore it must have had its own *ba*, an entity that could travel around in "sleep."

Logic further dictates that this *ba* would have had the same problem. It also needed two "bodies." One was the *ka*. But when the *ka* was "awake," that is, when the *ba* of the visible "body" was present in it because the "body" in the visible land was asleep, then the *ba* needed another abode, or it would be free floating, which was not an option.

If a living person was asleep and its *ba* was with the *ka*, this would leave the *ba* of the *ka* homeless, without a "body." Existence would then become partial, or non-complete, with a free-floating homeless *ba* searching in vain for a place to rest, someone or something to take up residence in. Such a part of personhood existed. The Ancient was not without logic. They did not invent an unfinished world. This *ka*/body of the *ba* was called an *akh*.

With the *akh* we have reached far into the invisible realm: closer to the source of everything, closer to "genesis" and the source of life. Closer to Atum, who transferred his life-force to his children, who in turn passed this "force" on to successive generations right up until the present people.

The *akh* is the *ba* of the former generation which finds its abode in the *ka* of the present generation. All these personal entities existed in the invisible world of the ancestors, that is, in the invisible realm of existence. These former generations, from Atum onwards, transmitted the life-force of Atum, to the present living "body"—the *ba* that enlivened the present *ka*/"body." In order to secure continued "genesis," Atum had to transmit his *ka* to his children, which he did by embracing them. Otherwise, his *ba* would have had nowhere to go. "Genesis," or the source of life, would have stopped right there.

Since the *akh* is the *ba* of the *ka*, and thus "lives" deep inside the invisible realm, Frankfort concludes that the *akh* was totally separate from humanity. He substantiates this by referring to a Pyramid Text which states: "!Akh to the sky, corpse into the earth," which leads him to surmise that the *akh* is always far away from the corpse, in contrast to the *ba*.

Frankfort concludes that the conception of the dead as *akh* is the vaguest and most detached of all the Ancient notions about "spirits." Still, as we would expect from an *akh* of a *ba*, Frankfort also thinks that this notion of personhood incorporates the *ake*s in the perennial cosmic order (2000 [1948]: 100–1).

We do know that everybody in Ancient Egypt participated in the world of the ancestors. We also know that every person's *akh* was related to the remote ancestry of a particular person's genealogy. Still, the *akh*'s had special relations to, and communicated with, the so-called gods, especially Re. Osiris was considered the supervisor of the *akhs* (Teeter 2011: 149–52), showing that we are deep inside the ancestors' realm.

We have now assembled the complete Ancient notion of personhood, consisting of *akh*, *ba*, *ka*, and a visible "body." This understanding is a social negotiation of living in two lands. These entities therefore had to be related to the cosmological system and its concepts and categories.

We are now in a position to draw a complete picture of Ancient Egyptian personhood according to their category system. All kinds of beings, from "gods" to humans, and probably all other matters and substances, simply lived in two lands (this is common in kinship-based societies):

Invisible land	Visible land
Ba (djet)	Body (nehen)
Akh (djet)	Ka (neheh)

We should remember that the *ba* also acted in the visible land. In the "body" or as a bird. Bodies and *ka*'s are perishable; *ba*'s are everlasting—given the right circumstances. Each person consisted of two equally constituted parts. The body was the outward appearance of a person in the land of living humans, an outside/outside while the *ba* is his/her inside life among the ancestors. The *ba* is, then, a person's inside/inside.

In the inside land, the *ba* was connected to a *ka*, a kind of "body" (like the body/statues of the gods in the visible realm) in the invisible realm, which acted as "a double," or as an inside/outside, to the inside/inside of the *ba*. To make any person complete, according to the categories used by the Ancient Egyptians, *djet—neheh*, the inside/outside *ka* needed its own inside/inside called the *akh*.

To simplify, every outside (*neheh*—transitional) needed an inside (*djet*—lasting), and *vice versa*. Moreover, these entities existed in two different lands. So, Ancient Egyptian personhood was a result of people living in "two lands." These combinations of the parts of personhood cover "gods," "kings," and humans, giving us a kind of existential template for Ancient Egypt.

How to translate *ka*, *ba*, *akh* and "body" is a moot point. It would take a thorough linguistic study conducted by a linguist well acquainted with Ancient Egyptian culture. Translating these "person-parts" as "double," "soul," and "spirit," respectively, makes no sense.

That said, this Egyptian model of personhood also evoked real horror among the Ancients. Given the right preparations, any person could live forever, as long as the corpse were conserved in the tomb, or supplied with a "stand-in" such as a statue. All the essential parts of personhood would then be intact and people could live on, although with some minor changes. Being a *ba*-bird is not exactly the same as having a body among the living.

However, the second component of personhood could also die, and people would experience a second death. The *ka*, a person's double/twin, could also die. For the *ka* to continue its existence, it needed the dead "body," or at least an imitation like a statue (such as those used by the "gods") in which it could continue to reside in the grave.

For various reasons, the preservation of the body could fail. People could lose their bodies in life. Then the *ba* would have nowhere to rest. Death would then be irreversible and permanent. This could happen if people were consumed by fire, eaten by dogs, or snatched by crocodiles (Tyldesley 2011: 179). Then there would be no body to preserve, and no abode for the *ba*.

People could also just have lived corrupt lives. Any dead person had to stand in front of a tribunal of "gods" headed by Osiris. This tribunal would weigh the heart of the deceased (the seat of the *ba*) against a feather, the feather being the lighter entity compared to a bad conscience. Failing this test, people faced a second death. This second death would follow the destruction of the corpse and the death of the *ka*. This was the plight of humans. This grave fate resulted from their cosmological order and its categories.

Even "Gods" related to each other as parts of the common model for personhood, the template, and the way its elements related to the categorical system. That is why Re traveled around the "cosmos" every day, and met up with Osiris at night. Together, they rejuvenated the "cosmos" by constituting two different but necessary aspects of this. They related to each other as the *neheh* and *djet* of existence in the invisible land, as Osiris (*djet*), the permanent one in his grave, and Re (*neheh*), the transitional one in his endless circuit. Horus is then "the body" of Osiris, through which he is able to travel between the two lands. All of these entities were brought into being by Atum who is the *ka* of Re, who is the *ba* of Osiris, whose body, Horus, rules the living:

So the world of the "gods" and the ancestry of Horus look like this:

Invisible land	Visible land
Osiris (*ka*)	Horus (*ba*)
Atum (*akh*)	Re (*ba*)

This combination of "gods" makes a direct link between Atum and Horus, and thereby authenticates his position as ruler of humankind. It made the rule of Horus indisputable. The Ancient world revolved around this constellation of "gods." This is a truly "animated" world, driven by personal "powers."

This particular organization is a symbolic ordering of the cosmos which, in turn, is a political negotiation of contemporary social organization and its status positions. It did not last. During the so-called First Intermediary Period, a profound upheaval shook the Pyramid Age. It collapsed. Royalty was swept away, and individual "kings" could no longer be relied upon, either in this life or in the hereafter (2000 [1948]: 103).

The major Ancient Egyptian trading partner, Byblos, and its neighboring countries were ransacked, and Egypt's trading partners disappeared over night. This collapse completely changed reproductive conditions in Egypt. Consequently, it also changed Egyptian social organization. "Kings," or living representatives of the ancestral world, fell out of fashion. "Kings" could no longer ensure the "cosmic" order. They had failed. Their world order had collapsed, and new practices had to be invented. Pharaohs no longer acted as intermediaries between the two lands—at least not in the same way. No more pyramids were built.

Ancient Egyptian cosmology determined their practices, their building strategies and all their pictorial renderings. They acted in their world. As they found it constituted. Since the pharaohs' relationships with the invisible world of the ancestors were the major factor in their power positions, pictorial (political) representations of the pharaohs made every possible effort to connect the ancestors to the pharaohs' "godly" positions. Including in the famous Narmer Palette.

Ancient Egyptians and the pharaohs apparently also had to perform the same "ritual" several times during the reign of long-lived pharaohs, as a political manifestation of their continued godly status. So the pharaohs performed the so-called *Heb-Sed* festival regularly, presumably to confirm their special relationship to the ancestral world.

Building pyramids was not, at any time, an idle pastime to keep peasants occupied during the slow periods in their agricultural cycles. It was a practice deemed necessary to keep the "cosmos" running. In addition, building these huge structures was an all too repetitive and resource-intensive practice to satisfy the whims of any single megalomaniac pharaoh. If the pharaohs were so concerned with being extraordinary, they would have preferred to erect their own individual monuments that would distinguish them from their predecessors (then they would have acted very modern). But instead, each pharaoh was compelled to build the same kind of mega-structure. This could only be due to a cultural necessity. Remarkably, the pharaohs built twenty-one of these structures in total.

Ancient ways of understanding the cosmos laid the foundation for the way the Egyptians behaved, and laid the groundwork for their cultural practices. Practices are culturally bound. They are not random, even though some may claim that they are. This does not mean that there cannot be political dissent or conflicting interests, but these contentions must transpire within a common framework of shared categories and concepts.

Social organization and social practices are complementary phenomena. Social organization is, in turn, based on the ongoing negotiation of the reproductive conditions of a given society. Up until the Old Kingdom, Egypt's glory was based on gold. The social negotiation of the distribution of gold determined Egypt's social organization, its kinship system and status positions in society. When the market for gold suddenly vanished with the collapse of Byblos, the Old Kingdom collapsed. Practices had to change.

Chapter 5

Ancient Practices

From a purely materialistic viewpoint, the gold in the Eastern Desert was the reason that there developed a social hierarchy in Upper Egypt in contrast to Lower Egypt who had no access to gold deposits. From early days, Ancient Egypt was the gold deposit of the ancient world. Gold were Ancient Egypt's main, if not only, export item. Gold was in high demand all over the Levant and the Mesopotamians were insatiable. The market seemed endless. In return, Egypt obtained a wide range of prestige-goods, from oil to cedar tree.

From early Badarian time groups of herders prospected gold in the Wadis leading into the Nile. Obviously not every family had the same access to the areas where the gold was located. This created a local elite group that was "internationally" connected and local herders/farmers who had to exchange local product to get the imported prestige goods that was necessary in social reproduction to celebrate special social events.

It all happened in Upper Egypt. That was where the gold was located. Nothing remotely similar transpired in Lower Egypt that mostly acted as trade-middlemen between Upper Egypt and the Levant and Mesopotamia. Being intermediaries seem not to have been a favorable situation for the evolution of steep hierarchical societies. Everybody in this area had very similar social situations.

Over time, the main centers of the gold deposit in Upper Egypt located near Naqada, Abydos and Hierakonpolis were united under one ruler, probably Narmer. With the later annexation of gold-rich Nubia there were only on leader of all the gold in the Nile Valley. With all these riches, Ancient Egypt evolved into the Old Kingdom with an extremely hierarchical social organization. Tremendously rich pharaohs had by now the means to build nearly whatever they wanted, while the common people toiled away. This was the age of the pyramids.

Such a social organization could only be expressed through a kinship system that distributed the resources between the different status groups, integrating local producers into an overall political structure based on exchange of prestige-goods for local products. Ancestry then became the major factor in determining position. Contemplations about how this kind of social organization came into being were negotiated in narratives about genesis.

In kinship-based societies position is a result of ancestry, and as such the tremendous power of the pharaohs could only be comprehended as stemming from direct descent from the remote ancestors, or what has been termed the first "god." Accordingly the pharaoh was considered semi-divine, and as an incarnation of the "gods" living among humans. He lived, so to speak, both among the "gods" and among humans. As such the world was divided into a land for the "gods" and one for humans. The pharaoh lived in both spheres at the same time, and was therefore able to communicate directly with the "gods."

This ability to live in two lands at the same time had to rest on a common principle uniting all Egyptian inhabitants into the same cosmos. Genesis explores this situation as well as the "kings" special position. It tells about how the world came to be divided into two spheres by introducing dead among the "gods" by the killing of Osiris by his brother Set. Osiris was nonetheless able to produce an heir that forever was the "king" of Egypt. From then on, the cosmos consisted of two lands. Everybody lived accordingly, having a "dream-identity" in the invisible land of the god and an "acting-identity" in the visible land of humans.

Living between two lands of existence in which the ancestors influenced the lives of the living and everything else, meant that people lived in an "animated" world, where "gods" could take abode in everything. Such a worldview determined the concepts and categories that the Ancient used to characterize their world.

Ancient Egyptians therefore did not have any concept of nature, biology or physics. They divided the beings and object into permanence, *djet* (as in the lives of "gods") and transients, *neheh* (as in the lives of humans). Everything had to combine these aspects, so that a *djet* was connected to a *neheh* in one realm and to their opposite in the other realm of existence.

This was clearly expressed in the Egyptian concept of personhood. This consisted of a body in the visible realm that had a *ba* in the invisible realm that in turn had its own body in the invisible realm called a *ka* that had its own *ba* called an *akh*. Thus, everyone had two "personalities," one living in each realm of existence, but where the *ba* was able to cross-over between the realms. Giving an existential experience of living in two lands simultaneously.

Having such an understanding of cosmos and such a concept of personhood determines how the world is experienced, and how people behave. It determines social practices. Practices has to conform to cosmology. Or else, people's actions become meaningless. Ancient Egyptian understanding of "the world" gave the rationale for the "king's titles" and "crowns," for every "art" expressions, for their so-called rituals and any form of constructions they made, such as "enclosures," "temples," and pyramids.

In this optic, and according to Ancient Egyptian cosmology, these were all ways of connecting with the "gods." Pictures were not just pictures; they were ways of communicating with the "gods." Making figures and palettes were not just symbolic devises of worship, but ways to invoke the "gods." Pyramids were not just graves, but essential meeting grounds for "gods" to ensure the continuation of the cosmos.

THE SYMBOLISM OF STATUS: "TITLES" AND "CROWNS"

Exchange between groups and status formation was expressed through a kinship system, but status also has to be symbolically elaborated. In accord with Ancient cosmology and concept of personhood the "kings" was able to live in the two realms of existence simultaneously, and consequently his "titles" and pictorial renderings, "crowns," had to reflect this duality. His position was cosmological determined.

However the "kings" position and his "titles" and "crowns" are often taken to reflect geo-political concerns, as expressing a uniting of Upper and Lower Egypt—"the two lands." This unification fixation is, inter alia, based on the Turin Royal Canon, the Abydos king list and the Palermo king list. On this list someone called Menes who is listed as having a double "title," thought by many to reflect that he unified the "Two Lands," founded the first dynasty. Unification is also believed to be the reason why the "Kings" are shown wearing two different "Crowns"—the Red Crown of Lower Egypt, and the White Crown of Upper Egypt. Such "crowns" have never been found, however.

As Lloyd points out "[t]he phrase "Upper and Lower Egypt" runs like a mantra through Ancient Egyptian studie" (2014: 158). Prior to such a unification, it is believed that the "King" only had a so-called Horus name that identified him with the falcon god Horus. The pictorial rendering of this "title" is a Falcon perched on top on some form of enclosure. In later times, this enclosure contained the "King's" name.

A common way to explain this imagery is for instance as follows:

> The symbolism of this title is very strong, as it expresses a close relationship between the earthly power of the King (the palace) and divine power of the celestial god Horus, the falcon who, from high above oversees the entire country and can strike at any prey below. (The Ancient Egypt Site 2014)

Obviously, and contrary to such interpretation, the duality in this "title" is between Horus (the "King") and the "Box" (grave/enclosure). It seems that this "title" like all the other "titles" for the "King," is a double constellation; a "falcon" and a "box" (grave/enclosure). Since this double "title", "Horus—box", was retained for a long time, it probably acted as a prototype for all later "titles," which then became extensions of its symbolism: a falcon and a grave/enclosure. To claim that this is simply the "King's" Horus name completely misses its symbolism and cultural significance.

"Kings" from the First Dynasty adopted a second title that was also written as a double entity: that is, the so-called *Nebty* name, also referred to as the "Two Ladies," Nekhbet (vulture) and Wadjet (cobra) (Wilkinson 2011: 46). This title is often interpreted according to the idiom of two lands being united. The vulture and cobra are then said to "represent" two goddesses, which in turn were "associated" with different towns:

> Nekhbet the vulture was associated with Nekheb (modern Elkab), a town opposite Nekhen in the heart of Upper Egypt. Wadjet the cobra was the goddesses of Dep, one of the twin towns which made up the important Delta city Per-Wadjet (modern Tell el-Fara'in); she therefore stood for Lower Egypt. (Wilkinson 2011: 46)

Leaving aside the problem that these places play neither any important role in Upper nor Lower Egypt, and that this interpretation therefore seems far reached, by relating the two creatures to localities in Upper and Lower Egypt the "title" came to represent the unification of the two lands. This is believed to be further verified by the fact that Nekhbet (vulture) is often depicted wearing the "White Crown" and Wadjet (cobra) wearing the "Red Crown." As a result, the "title" reflects supposed geo-political events instead of cosmological meaning, as we would normally expect in a kinship-based society.

However, this was the time of the "striker" and "fighter" pharaohs of the First Dynasty, who took their staff and servants with them into their graves, or buried them along the walls of their ceremonial enclosures. Moreover, it does not take much imagination to relate these images of so-called retainer graves to the doings of cobras and vultures, killers and devourers. These would seem to be fitting symbols for such pharaohs, evoking an imagery that seems better suited to what was thought to be their cultural schema. Of course, the characteristics of these creatures would be depicted as "goddesses"—but in actuality, we have no knowledge of what these creatures meant to the Ancient Egyptians. It is all based on guesswork, and speculative associations.

A third "title" consists of two Egyptian words, *nesu bity*, which has been literally translated as "he of the reed and bee" (Wilkinson 2011: 47) (an equally odd constellation). Wilkinson finds that the precise derivation of this title is obscure. He writes, "On one level the reed may have symbolized Upper Egypt and the bee Lower Egypt" (2011: 47). "Crowns" were adopted at the same time as the third title. In relation to the "crowns" Wilkinson writes, "The adaptation of the red and white crowns was part of the same process [as with the 'titles']" (2011: 46).

Since the so-called Horus name also consist of a double entity, we should probably use the same logic for this "title" as a guideline to account for the *Nebty* and the *nesu bity* "titles." In this double version the Horus "title" would translate as "He of the Bird and the Box," or maybe more appropriate "He of the Falcon-*ba* and the Netherworld," more befitting to a person striding the two realms of existence. This interpretation is however never done, probably because the "King" is known to have had this title a long time before unification, and therefore such an interpretation would obliterating the idea of unification as the main event in Ancient history.

What all this shows is that we are not apprised of the Ancient Egyptian category system in which these seemingly different creatures can be reconciled to characterize one person. At any rate, they must have been vastly different from contemporary Western categories.

Wilkinson also acknowledges that there might be a problem with these interpretations of the "titles" and "crowns." He writes, "The red crown can be traced back to the rock art of the Eastern Desert . . . in the Wadi Qash" (2003: 81). Alas, in the wrong part of the country and at a time long before any pharaohs ruled a united Egypt.

Also, the first time we are introduced to the "White Crown" is on the Narmer palette, on which Narmer also bears the "Red Crown" on the opposite site of the palette. Narmer ruled just before the first dynasty. The "Red Crown" seems to be much older, or at least there are finds from much earlier periods depicting this "crown." As Rice writes,

> [C]onfusingly, the earliest representations of the red crown, traditionally identified with the northern Kingdom . . . is on a pottery shed recovered from a southern site, Naqada, and quite firmly dated to the Naqada I period, in the middle of the fourth millennium, c. 3500 BC. (Rice 1991: 112)

This is long before there was any indication of a unified kingdom, and also in the wrong region! And a long way away from the town Dep, Wadjet the cobra was the goddesses.

As Rice continues, "[T]his is rather disconcerting; it inevitably calls again into question the reality or otherwise of the northern Kingdom and whether it really existed at all" (1991: 112). How, or why, the "red crown" ended up representing the North is, as he writes, "speculation, nothing more" (1991: 112). To complicate matters, Lloyd writes, "[U]pper and Lower Egypt very rarely figure as discrete administrative entities in their own right" (2014: 158). And in relation to a conquest of Lower Egypt by the southerners, it seems that

> the movement of the Naqada population into Lower Egypt began many centuries before the time of Narmer and that it did not appear to have been accompanied by warfare. (Romer 2012: 143)

We do not even know what the "crowns" were made of. Romer has an ingenious suggestion. Since the pot shed with the depiction of the "red crown" was found "close to some native sources of copper ore,

> [it] might suggest that this crown may once have been made of thin sheets of that red-shining metal . . . the White Crown appears to have been a more recent innovation than the Red Crown of Lower Egypt. In life, it may have been made of basketwork and plaster. (2013: 141)

However, if the "Red Crown" was made of copper, it is hard to explain how these crowns disappeared off the face of the Earth. No trace of them has ever been found. One would think that if pharaohs had been wearing these crowns for thousands of years, they would have left some kind of trace in the archeological record. As we know from Tutankhamun's coffin, the pharaohs did not even take these "crowns" with them into their graves. Since there is no real evidence to prove these assumptions, we must conclude that "crowns" and "titles" probably meant something different to the Ancient Egyptians.

What could these "crowns" be? One solution to this conundrum is that they never existed as physical entities. Let me give you a hint, as Rice writes, "representations of Osiris . . . are always depicted wearing the white crown of the Archaic Upper Egyptian Kings" (1991: 54). Osiris was the king of "the afterlife" or the "Netherworld." He is clearly a dead man wearing a "white crown." To understand the significance of this observation, we have to probe into Ancient Egyptian cosmology, their worldview, and the forces they believed moved the world around them.

To sum up: From Pre-Dynastic times, a Falcon perched on top of a box represented the pharaoh. Then we have the *Nebty* name, consisting of a cobra and a vulture. After this the next "title" is the *nesu bity* that consists of a reed and a bee. Next is the pharaoh's Golden Horus name that also clearly consists of a double entity, a Falcon and a symbol for gold.

We have to link all these "titles" and the "crowns" to Ancient cosmology. If we pursue our skepticism about the uniting of Upper and Lower Egypt as explanations for these "titles" and "crowns" we notice that there is a clear repetition of form in which all "titles" consist of a duality, but with different content. In the first "title," called the pharaoh's Horus name, we have a

Falcon and a "box" (probably an enclosure or a grave, see about this constellation later). The latter probably represents the "ancestors" (or "God"), and from later times we know that it was Osiris, King of the "Netherworld." He is always depicted wearing the "White Crown," while Horus always wears the "Red Crown."

Horus is King of the living (realm); Osiris (ancestor) is King of the dead (realm). In other words, Horus is King of all that is visible, a world of appearances, while Osiris is king of an unseen world of ancestors that nonetheless influences the world of the living. Together, they depict an Upper realm and a Nether realm of existence, and the two "crowns" represent this difference. Since no traces of such "crowns" have ever been found, they must be artistic means used in pictograms to depict the roles assumed by the "King" and others at different ceremonial occasions.

We can now line up all the titles according to how they relate to the Upper and Nether realm:

Upper Realm	Nether realm
Red Crown	White Crown
Horus	"Box" (Osiris)
Cobra	Vulture
Reed	Bee
Horus	Gold

These constellations therefore probably indicate that the "King" in different (socially) capacities was able to transcend this division between the two realms, the Upper and Nether realm, since he is depicted using symbols from both realms.

It is a little tricky to place the "reed" and the "bee," and maybe we should refrain from trying until further evidence is found. In the last title, "The Golden Horus name," we again have Horus in the Upper Realm, and because gold was considered the substance of the gods, it represents the Nether Realm. It is, however, unclear why these different entities were chosen, since we do not know how Ancient Egyptians classified plants, beings and objects.

These "titles" and "crowns" do not reflect some form of geo-politics and a union of Upper and Lower Egypt. Unification seems to be less important than assumed. "Titles" are cosmological, as one would expect from a kinship-based society. "Crowns" were merely an artistic way to depict which realm those acting in the pictograms belonged to. Just like in the first plate in the "Book of the Dead" where Isis and Nephthys are shown, depicted exactly alike, on either side of Osiris-Re in a posture of adoration. "Like most Egyptian goddesses, they are distinguishable only by the attributes . . . that they wear on their heads" (Faulkner and Goelet 2015: 164)! This differs from the

"King" case, in which the same person performs different "roles," which are artistically represented by "Crowns."

INVOKING THE *BA*

Ancient Egyptian practices are all too often written off as based on magical worldview, and as such we are made familiar through know concepts with an otherwise completely other worldview with it whole array of improbably "gods" and ritualistic practices. Beware, however, that the Ancient thought system was one of the most long lived civilization of Earth, and that they were able to make building constructions that are still awe inspiring today—and still to a large part incomprehensible. It was not all "magic." Much understanding hinge on understanding Ancient concept of personhood, and the way the *ba* was invoked.

Superficially, it might seem that Egyptian practices were inextricably linked with "magic." Ancient Egypt has "long been considered a land of mystery and magic" (Wenke 2009: 9). Ancient Egypt has even been described as the "mother of magicians" (Rankine 2006: 7). Rankine boldly states, "Magic was not considered strange or eccentric, but was part of daily life as food or drink" (2006: 7). Pinch follows suit, writing that "the evidence for ancient Egyptian magic spans thousands of years" (Pinch 2006: 9).

This perceived prevalence of Egyptian "magic" stems from what is seen as "spells" (Pinch 2006: 9), for example, in The Pyramid Texts, and in healing practices recorded on long lists of "medical papyri" in which drugs and procedures are interpreted as being supplemented with "magical spells" (Goelet 2015: 157). All too often this leads to "the image of Egypt as a source of occult knowledge" (Pinch 2006: 9).

This interpretation of Ancient practices hinges on our understanding of "magic." What is "magic"? (A remark: Boldly stated it is a term Westerner uses to describe practices that they do not understand. To make matters worse they back this assumption up with the statement that "magic" is underpinned by "ritual" (practices that are seen as having no real results), and that all these are by the natives shrouded in some mythological thoughts). To understand "magic," many Western scholars work under the premises laid out by early anthropologists and their *definitions of magic*. Magic is by a common definition to use spells to "coerce gods and supernatural beings to perform" Goelet 2015: 156) according to ones wish.

This definition of magic worked as long as the anthropological subject remained silent. They are not anymore. They have become anthropologists themselves. In a world of globalized scholarship, it seems that the translation of a multiplicity of life-forms into universalist European categories is problematic (Escobar and Ribeiro 2006: 4).

In this light, the Indian anthropologist Momin (2001) calls for a critical reappraisal of the theoretical and methodological baggage of Western anthropology. According to Momin, such a project requires "investigation into the relevance, and utility of conceptual categories and methodological approaches in the traditions of the non-Western world" (p. 60). From an Indian point of view, it seems that the cultures of the former subjects of colonialism and anthropology have "been subjected to a disgraceful generalization" and that anthropologists produced descriptive accounts of quaint customs and beliefs, with the result that traditional thought was "branded as a collection of empty concepts" (Saraswati 2001: 3–4).

We should take this criticism of standard anthropological parlance serious. Also in the case of Ancient Egypt, ancient Egyptian did not have a concept of "religion" and therefore did not have any "supernatural" beings that could be summoned with "spells." Since they did not have a word for "spell," they could not cast one (or else you are claiming that the Egyptians lived a Western cosmology in bad faith). They must have (at least thought) that they were doing something else. Practice is embedded in local cosmology, and it reflects the local notion of personhood.

To emulate "The Book of the Dead" (*Coming Forth by Day*), *What does it mean?*: The local notion of personhood acts as a template for the way people behave in the world. *Otherwise said*: Personhood determines how people perceive their surrounding world and the forces they thing makes the world go around. *Otherwise said*: All kinds of practices conform to some kind of a template of existence that organizes the everyday world of people, its concepts and categories. Everywhere. Nobody can see his or her own magic. People can build pyramids and skyscrapers anyhow.

According to Ancient Egyptian cosmological system personhood consisted of a double entity with one part living in Light-land and one part living in the Netherworld. Each land/world had equal status for the individuals.

In the temples, we have already encountered how the Egyptian understood the relationship between a "symbol" and its referent, as a relationship between the *ba* of the "gods" and a *ka* provided by a "statue." As Assman also observes, *"The statue is not the image of the deity's body, but the body itself"* (Assmann 2001: 46, *italic* in original). It does not "represent" his form, but rather gives him form. These receptacles/Statues were not made, they were born. (Assmann 2001: 46). "'Deities' were no fictions, but genuine powers" (Assmann 2001: 47).

This relationship between "statues" and "gods" expresses *the* general Ancient principle between all kinds of "symbols" and referents. All kinds of "representations" were *ka*s for the "god's" *ba*s to embody. Then, every "image" was a living being and/or performing scenarios. These "images" and scenarios made the "gods" or even the cosmos come alive. Images were made to make things happen.

Images did not picture "gods" or portray "stories"; they were the "gods" or the enactment of the "stories." Even speech was a possible *ka* for the "gods" *ba* to enlighten in (words were no neutral), "amulets" likewise, hieroglyphs, "voodoo-dulls," and so on. These were all ways of invoking the *ba*s of the "gods."

While the Egyptians had no word for "religion," many scholars claim that they had a concept for "magic" (maybe because magic is thought to belong to a more primitive pre-religious worldview), called *heka*. Goelet claims that according to the Coffin Texts, one of the first acts of the creator when he fashioned the universe was to create magic, his eldest son, named *Heka* (forget Atum, ancient ideas of genesis are not very consistent). Sometime after this, the creator entrusted both gods and humanity with magic as one of his "great deeds." *Heka*, then, was the deity personifying magic (Goelet 2015: 156). With *heka*, both people and gods can make words and wishes effective. *Heka* can be used to create or destroy, protect or (Rankine 2006: 13) harm (Goelet 2015: 156).

As Rankine describes *Heka*'s abilities:

> One of the titles of the god Heka was the one who consecrates imagery, referring to the ability of the god to empower creative thoughts and actions and translate them into their physical equivalents in the physical world. So Heka was also perceived as the animating and manifesting force of every ritual act. In this context, heka is thus both intent and action: the cause, the act and the effect (Rankine 2006: 13). [Heka] it empowered man to create using words and actions, mirroring the sun god's creative universe. Heka can be seen as the creative force of life-giving energy connecting the objects, links and symbols of life with the universe, like a subtle tapestry of energy. (Rankine 2006: 12)

Then *Heka* is the personification of magic:

> Heka was a god, indeed he was the god of magic. Or, perhaps it would be more correct to say he was magic, being the divine personification of magic. (Rankine 2006: 13)

It is not that simple. As it turns out, *Heka* conformed to the way personhood was conceived by the Ancients. We therefore have to turn to the way *Heka* is described by the Ancients. In the Coffin text the so-called spell 261 reads:

I am he whom the Lord of all [Re] made before duality had yet come into being . . . the son of him who gave birth to the universe . . . I am the protection of that which the Lord of all has ordained . . . I am he who gave life to the Ennead of the gods . . . come to take my position that I may receive my dignity. Because to me belonged the universe before you gods had come into being. You have come afterwards because I am Heka. (Rankine 2006: 13)

Also, the Ancient positioned *Heka* squarely inside their understanding of personhood. In the "Book of The Heavenly Cow," Re declares:

I am the one who made heaven and who established it in order to place the ba's of the gods within it. I shall be with them for eternity which time begets. My ba is Heka. It is older than it [time] . . . the ba of Re is in Heka throughout the entire land. (Rankine 2006: 15)

It seems that *Heka* was the creative power of Re. So, *Heka* conformed to Ancient personhood. No magic. Only the result of the Ancient concept of personhood that made it possible to summoning the *ba* of Re. We can relax; the Ancient Egyptians did not have a secret formula for magic. They acted within their worldview.

Heka was the first *ba*, the creative power that sprung into being by its own force. In addition, people could call upon it. To be able to call on the *ba* of the primordial being, the sun Re, and have him act in your favor in the invisible land, the Netherworld, the Duat, would be a destiny changer. It looks as magic—at least seen, years later from another world.

Ancient Egyptians did not try to hide their conception of the cosmos. Every free space was plastered with pictures and texts telling about what the Ancients thought went on in their world. They also made long descriptions on papyri guiding their own people through what they thought was the "after-lives"—the world of *ba*s. Therefore, it is not for lack of information that it is so difficult to understand Ancient Egyptian society.

STRADDLING THE TWO REALMS/ LANDS OF EXISTENCE

The next part of this exposition of Ancient Egyptian lives and practices are to some extent superfluous. It is just a repetition of the cultural logic already laid out. However, when we are trying to understand Ancient Egyptian life and expression, let us be clear about it: They had *no symbols!* Everything could be a vehicle for a *ba*. Everything was a living entity. This is our starting point. In this way, Ancient Egyptians were very practical, that is, within their worldview, and they went to great lengths to inform the surrounding world about their doings.

Another word of caution before we start to read Old Egyptian expressive practices in whatever form or material they found an outlet. In present-day kinship based societies, in which people also live contemporaneously in two realms of existence with one part among the ancestors and one part among the living, these realms have equal status and realities for the people involved. What transpires for a person while "asleep" among the ancestors has the same importance as what s/he experiences while being "awake" among the living. Sometimes even more so, since these "dream" happenings sometimes take place among the remote ancestors. When people in these kinds of societies are telling about their experiences, be sure to ask what part of personhood was involved (or you will just be confused and probably explain it away as "magic").

Such questions we cannot ask the Ancient Egyptians. But in their pictograms, they had to conveying to the spectators in which realm the action they were watching took place with some kind of "sign", for example, "crowns." Due to the idea, that people had a double in the Afterlife, those living here, the dead, was pictured as living.

We have to realize that every image, statue or structure in Ancient Egypt was a way of calling the "cosmos" into being by providing a "body" for the *ba* of a god, or several gods at the same time. All these "representations" should be read according to Ancient cosmology and personhood. These different forms of images narrate that the world consisted of two lands and that every kind of being (tree, animal, rock, etc.) and persons lived divided between its two spheres. Images were used as *kas* either for the gods to enliven or for the deceased *bas* to take abode in.

This presentation of cosmos is extracted from the Pyramid Texts and the text *Going Forth by Day*. These are relatively late texts, but they must be based on some previous considerations about genesis, cosmos, its categories and forms of personhood. Basic understanding of symbolism probably did not change much throughout Ancient Egyptian history. Content can change but the basic relationships between "symbol" and referent were part of a long lasting cosmology in which everybody lived in two realms of "reality" contemporaneously.

There is no doubt, that the "rulers" of Ancient Egypt became increasingly wealthy and powerful propelling Pre-dynastic Egypt into what has also been called the 0th dynasty, by having subsumed the power of Naqada, Abydos, and This under one "ruler" and afterward by annexing Nubia. It seems that in Pre-dynastic time to be wealthy was a question of ancestry, and this was lavishly demonstrated in progressively greater grave monuments throughout Pre-dynastic Egypt finding a preliminary culminating in 0th Dynasty, where the graves had all the accruements of life, to be used by the deceased in the afterlife.

Rulers were buried like their fellow community members, although in vastly more elaborate graves. In this context, they were like other human beings at the time. There seems to have been a slight difference in burial traditions between Abydos and Saqqara. In Saqqara, the tombs are based on a conception of the deceased as living on after death in a building resembling his ordinary house in life. In Abydos the burial conception, seem to have been based on a funeral mound like the primal mound. Inside they consisted of a burial chamber and some storerooms (Verner 2001: 24). Such graves indicate that the "ruler" was a descendent from the earliest ancestors (primordial "gods") and therefore was "merely" a mortal incarnation of the first ancestral lineage.

"Rulers" were not yet "divine" or living ancestors, that is, the *ba* of a "god." At this time, their *ba* must have been constituted in the same way as with ordinary people. It could travel in the Afterlife in sleep. Maybe the "rulers" at this time had special abilities to *communicate* with the ancestors in the invisible realm, but these graves indicates that they did not yet have the status of being able to live simultaneously in both realms of existence.

However, the momentous changes that transpired at the time of the 0th Dynasty had to be followed with adjustment to the Ancient cosmology and the conceptualization of the "ruler." We know from the Pyramid Texts and the Papyrus of Ani how this came to be realized in later time, but precious little about how this cosmology came into being. However, the thoughts expressed in these texts must have had some kind of forerunners. There are at least two such ideological/cosmological forerunners: the Narmer Palette and the Enclosures, the last one being precursors of the pyramids.

THE NARMER PALETTE

The Narmer Palette is by many seen as the ultimate expression of the unification of Upper and Lower Egypt (e.g., Midant-Reynes 2000), and that he accomplice it by force. Since they believe that it was a conquest, they see victims and surrender on the Palette.

However, archeologically there seems to have been no subjugation of Lower Egypt by military force, and therefore no victims and surrender. Most of the "symbolism" have been seen before and after (e.g., the "smiting" scene), and some of the interpretations presupposes unification as the origin of the Palette's iconography (e.g., the serpopards). Is seems that the Palette is telling another story.

Recent archeological research made by a German expedition making excavation at the cemetery at Umm el-Qaab, near Abydos, suggests that Narmer was not the first "king" to unite Upper and Lower Egypt. From the graves, it appears that there were no political or economic break at the time of Narmer.

Instead, the graves at Umm el-Qaab show a clear continuity between the 0th and the First Dynasty. So the era of unification had already begun centuries earlier (Verner 2001: 15).

This observation do not make the Palette less enigmatic, and we will probably never understand its full message. It is all too prototypical in its hieroglyphic content and its iconography. The content of the Palette clearly belong to an earlier tradition than The Pyramid Texts and the text and iconography of the Ani papyrus (from which we have our version of "genesis"). It has a whole other set-up, but it is tampering with the same ideas of how the ruler is connecting the two realms of existence.

The palette has been described and presented far and wide, and also in the historical chapter of this book. No need to repeat the basic description of the Palette here. On the top of both sides flanking the *serekh* of Narmer, Hathor is looking at us. Her presence means that she was the "god" that was supposed to embody the Palette. It was a *ka* for her *ba*. Her presence must be significant.

Hathor's qualities then become of the outmost importance. Hathor's name means "the domain of Horus." She was the golden goddess who helped women given birth (a kind of fertility), and she helped the dead to be reborn, and the cosmos to be renewed (a kind of "genesis"). She eased the transition from death to new life. She ruled the underworld from where she emerged to punish those who behaved unjustly on earth. She was the goddess of all precious metals, gemstones, gold silver, copper, turquoise, lapis-lazuli, and faience. Furthermore, she was the goddesses of foreign lands and their products (Pinch 2002: 137–9).

These abilities clearly linked her to the ancient prestige economy, in which precious products were traded with foreign lands, an ability that involved the power to act in both realms of existence. Prestige product being a kind of "life force" in the Ancient social organization based on ancestry.

Each side of the palette consists of so-called registers, linked narratives. On the side with the hollow grinding spot and underneath Hathor, there are three registers. On the other side and underneath Hathor, there are only two.

On the hollow side, there are first a procession on the left side with Narmer wearing the "sign" of Horus on his head, followed by his "sandal bearer." On the right side, there are ten decapitated men lying on the ground. Since the procession and the decapitated people are in the same register, most observers see the procession approaching the men on the ground as either sacrificial victims of Narmer or his subjugated enemies from the North.

There are no writings to explain the Narmer Palette or any other Pre-Dynastic palettes (Tyldesley 2011: 69), which gives a large room for interpretations. Different observers see different "stories" in the different registers of the palettes. Tyldesley, for instance, sees the king marching with a troop of soldiers whose standards may represent the symbols of the newly unified Egyptian provinces. A person in front of Narmer, a bit smaller but larger than the "soldiers," she sees as his scribe, who she thinks is essential to record the king's victories. In front of these, she sees ten unfortunate victims of war (Tyldesley 2003: 35).

Verner sees Narmer wearing the crown of Lower Egypt in a cortege of men bearing standards with the symbols of the provinces of the victorious Upper Egyptian coalition, viewing executed enemies (2001: 17). In these two short descriptions, the standards are either thought to be symbols of a newly unified Egypt, or representing the victorious provinces of Upper Egypt.

In contrast, Allan interprets the figure walking in front of Narmer, as his vizier, and then goes on to identify the standards:

> The four standards preceding Narmer appear on the Narmer and Scorpion Mace-heads as two falcons with flags, Wepwawet and the placenta. They are identified with the Predynastic rulers the "Followers of Horus" named in the Turin Canon, and may refer to Thinite Royalty or ancestor cults. (Allan 2014: 54)

In this interpretation, the procession is therefore not associated with warfare.

On the overall look of the procession, Narmer is definitely not taking part in celebrating a war victory, and there is no indication of a battlefield. The beheaded and bound men "in front" of the procession seems like a scene all to itself, dead and beheaded to be sure, but these "victims" may "only" relate to the "headline" of prototype hieroglyphs above them, and therefore not directly related to the Narmer procession.

Above the beheaded men, we find a door, a bird, a boat and a falcon with a harpoon. Generally interpreted as "The door of Horus," as an entry or exit point to the foreign land to the north and to Mesopotamia (Allan 2014: 60). Horus is walking in the procession, but he is also flying through the "Gate of Horus" above the decapitated victims. He is in two places at the same time! So maybe the procession is not linked to the victims.

In the middle of the Palette on the same side, there are two so-called ser-popards with entwined necks, held in leaches by two differently looking men. Having discarded unification as a one off happening at this point in history, the serpopards can no longer be seen as a sign of unification of Upper and Lower Egypt. Others interpret Serpopards, as the "chaos" that reigned beyond Egypt's borders (Wikipedia 2018). This interpretation would make sense relative to the presence of "The Gate of Horus" leading to the foreign lands beyond. At the bottom, we see a bull (Narmer?) goring a town and a victim from this attack.

At the other side of the palette, Hathor is still presiding over the scenario transpiring below. Here we again have Narmer followed by his servant. This time Narmer is wearing the sign of "Osiris" on his head. He is "smiting" (or taking a man in oath) a person kneeling in front of him. To the right is a Falcon holding a man in a leash. This man has a body that look like the hieroglyph for "land." It has stems growing on the back.

Such "smiting scenes" are seen before. We find one on a painted vessel from Naqada and one in the Painted tomb. We also find this motive on an ivory label of Den (already mentioned). This label gives some further clue to what is going on because it is followed with some (hard to read) texts. On left side of Den, the hieroglyph "upraised hands" are depicted, generally translated as *ka*. To the other side, Den is identified as performing "the first time of smiting the East(erners?)" by a hieroglyphic inscription (Allan 214: 17). So, Den's *ka* are "smiting" the Easterners (in the land of chaos). Underneath, there is a register with two fleeing or dying persons.

It is tellingly that on the necropolis seals of Den and Qaa their predecessors are given the title "Horus Khenti-Amentiu," starting with "Horus Khenti-Amentiu Narmer. Khenti-Amentiu means "Foremost of the Westerners" or "Chief of the Westerners" (Wilkinson 1999: 288), a title that can also be translated as "Chief of the Netherworld," linking Westerners and Netherworld. Thereby the "Chief of the Westerners" are in collaboration with Hathor, the goddesses of precious objects and foreign lands.

Another short digression, going back to the discussion of the "king's" many titles. Right from the start, these titles were based on a double entity. At this time, it was as Horus and Khenti-Amentiu. This is also, what is depicted in the *serekh*: a Falcon (Horus) sitting on an enclosure/grave (Khenti-Amentiu). It therefore is abundantly clear that the "kings" had double "titles" long before any assumed unification.

Nevertheless, by combining Egypt's reproductive conditions (trading gold for prestige goods) and Ancient cosmology (existence divided between two realms), a possible reading of the Narmer Palette could be as follows.

On the side with the hollow in the Palette: Horus Narmer (indicated by the sign on his head) is collecting tax/tribute, which means that he is exchanging prestige goods for local product needed for the survival of his growing court. His scribe walk along in the procession, ready to take notes of the transactions. Standard-bearers shows Horus Narmer's credentials. They are "The Followers of Horus" (see below).

> Until well into the First Dynasty Egyptian rulers had no permanent residence. In the biennial "Horus-procession" they crossed the whole country with their retinue, in order to collect taxes, administer justice, and show themselves to the people. (Verner 2001: 17)

As we saw earlier, Marka's grave gives us insight into how the tribute system worked at the end of the first dynasty. At this early date, the "king" went on annual trips to collect his tribute in return for some forms of prestige goods (wine, oil, etc.) (Romer 2013: 255).

To obtain the prestige goods necessary to collect tribute Horus Narmer, in his bird shape, his *ba*, is sailing through "The Gates of Horus" into the land of chaos of the Westerners who are living beyond the desert (the section of the serpopards). Every land beyond in the west, the place of the setting sun, was a part of the Netherworld. Narmer is entering the Netherworld. Here, and in the form of a bull, he gore a town probably to obtain his much-needed products.

On the other side of the Palette: On entering the Horus gate, Narmer's *ba* is leaving many victims in his steps. Having sailed through "The Gates of Horus" and into (a kind of) Netherworld Narmer Khenti-Amentiu, his *ka* takes over, smiting his way through the foreign territory. He is fighting like Re when his is sailing through the Netherworld during nighttime:

> Greetings Re, when you arise, Atum at your beautiful setting! . . . The rebel has fallen, his arms are bound. The knife has penetrated his vertebra. . . . You pass the sandbank of the Sea of knives, your enemies are felled. (Assmann 2001: 105)

Narmer Khenti-Amentiu (Narmer chief of the Westerners) was clearly able to act in the Netherworld, also in foreign lands. These adventures into the land of the Westerners (part of the Netherworld) make it possible for him to obtain his needed trade goods. Having fought for his goods, we see the result on the right side of Narmer Horus, his *ba* in the form of a Falcon; control the landowning population of Egypt. By smiting the Westerners, Narmer is able to provide "life-force" to the Egyptian communities. He becomes the *ba* of the peasants (the landowners), giving them their "life-force."

"Smiting the Westerners" shows the "Kings" being able to travel in the chaos of the Netherland beyond the border, securing the prestige goods. Still, at this time is seems probably that Narmer was not divine—he was buried in an ordinary high status grave—but he was the living descendent of Horus.

So, both his *ba* and *ka* was acting for him. The *ba* flew into the "land beyond" and it enlightened in the people of the land providing them with "life-force," as illustrated by the Falcon holding the land people in a leach. Having flown into the "land beyond" his *ka* was acting in this part of the Netherworld.

We may therefore surmise that the so-called white crown at this time "just" represented the rulers *ka*, and that the so-called red crown identified the ruler as Horus. Only later did the white sign on the head of the "smiting" person become the sign for Osiris, when cosmology turned and made him into the "king" of the Netherworld.

Narmer, like all the rest of Upper Egypt's, ruler knew that his power was dependent on his vast gold reserves used to be exchanged for prestige goods with the foreign land in the West. In turn, he traded these imported goods internally for local product that provided the sustenance for his growing court. Thereby he traded the substance (gold) of the gods for food (tribute), via the lands in the West.

The only way he could show this foreign relation was by the "smiting scene" showing his force in the Netherworld among the "gods." In reality, he subdued the foreigners with gold, that is, with his gods. This is the reason why Hathor is "overseein" the Palette, being the goddesses of precious metal and of foreign lands.

Taken together, Narmer portrayed himself to act as both *ka* and *ba*, shown stylistically with the white and red headgear. Thereby he showed that he was able to straddle and live in the two lands simultaneously. This is the first time we see a depiction of a leader acting in both realms of existence at the same time. Newfound wealth at Narmer's time, seem to have produced a new conception of the leader. He was now more than a mere mortal, but he was still buried as one.

So what happened to the unification of the Upper and Lower Egypt? It was probably accomplice by other means, and over a longer period. Forging alliances through marriages would be an obvious choice. This would bring an increasing number of Lower Egyptians into the orbit of the Upper Egyptian prestige economy. There are strong indications that Narmer married a northern "princes" by the name Neith-Hotep from Sais (Tyldesley 2003: 39), thus being among those who instigated alliances with the north and thereby integrating these groups into the southern kinship system.

At this time, one of the pressing concerns of the ruler must have been to lure more landowning matri-lineages into the prestige-good system by making marriage alliances (the political game in kinship based societies). This process would mean that the southern kinship system was gradually implemented in Lower Egypt who up until this point had lived relatively independent of the social system in Upper Egypt. Upper Egyptians would forge alliances through marriages, not wage war. Unification by marriage.

Narmer needed more resources to keep up the sustenance of a growing elite with an increasingly lavishly lifestyle. He needed more arable land, and therefore he had to integrate Lower Egypt into the kinship system, so that the Northerners both acted as middlemen in trade and suppliers of agricultural resources.

THE ENCLOSURE

The ideological change towards the leaders being able to live simultaneously in the two realms meant that graves were no long enough to display their power. Graves were meant to "live," in the Afterlife. Having leaders that transcended this dichotomy called for new measures. Graves were supplemented with "enclosures." Enclosures are very large square constructions with white, high and thick walls, and with retainer graves around them, mimicking the graves of the rulers.

Most of the "kings" after Narmer and at least two from the Second Dynasty have built enclosures at Abydos, but none of these were built after the Second Dynasty. It has been suggested that they were built as arenas for the performance of the royal funerary ceremonies, but the sheer size suggest that they were built for something else. Arnold suggests that they should be seen as "architecture for the next world," that on the Palermo Stone were called "fortress of the gods" (Arnold 1997: 34).

From seal impressions, the identity of each enclosure has been identified. Here enclosures are depicted as rectangular fortified constructions surrounding the name of individual buildings. These are called:

"the companion of the gods" of "King" Djer
"the seats of the gods" of "King" Den
"the mound of the gods" of King Qa'a
"the house of natron for the gods" of an unknown predecessor of "King" Ninetjer
"the house of Horus/nurse of the god" of "King" Ninetjer
"libations of the gods" of "King" Djoser
"procession of the gods" probably of "King" Sekhemkhet. (Arnold 1997: 34)

We immediately notice that if unification had played a significant role at this time, and after Narmer, it did not leave any imprint on the names of the enormous construction. It is all cosmological.

In 1988, O'Connor excavated one of the larger enclosures belonging to Khasekhemwy:

> We are fairly sure that what once stood here was a large mound made of sand and gravel; it was covered with a brick skin, of which this brickwork is the lowest and only surviving piece. Khasekhemwy's mound rose above the ground surface of the enclosed area and was visible to any one who entered that enclosure. (O'Connor 1991: 7)

These enclosures housed "The Primeval Mound." They all seem to have been the gathering places for groups of gods

> who were predominantly divine powers who appeared in animal shapes. Collectively, the powers were known as . . . the Followers of Horus. (Arnold 1997: 34)

These followers were the adherents of the "King" in his earthly manifestation of the ancient sky and falcon god (Arnold 1997: 23). These followers had shrines around Egypt from where they undertook boat journeys along the Nile

to the enclosures arriving with standards or flags from the different provinces
to gather in the "fortress." Those

> fortresses stood at the west bank of the Nile, so the visitors would arrive from
> the east, at a quay long the Nile or a canal. These boat journeys were apparently
> linked to the collection of "taxes"/tribute, so that boats led by "gods" arrived at
> the enclosures with their treasures. (Arnold 1997: 6)

Furthermore:

> During the lifetime of the king the gods apparently assembled in the fortress
> of the gods to take part in the distribution of the incoming commodities and to
> establish contact with the king, whereby the king would provide the gods with
> offerings and a cultus and they would "follow" him as his powerful adherents.
> (Arnold 1997: 37)

Enclosures seem to represent a further development in tax collecting after
Narmer. On his Palette, we see Narmer in a procession travelling around the
country to collect taxes, while his *ba* is flying through The Gates of Horus
into the chaotic Netherworld of the Westerners, his *ka* smiting them along the
way to obtain the prestige goods needed for his position.

Now we also see what has been termed "boat burials," also know from
later times. During O'Connor's excavations in October 1991, his team found
twelve boat pits:

> Each boat grave, when complete, had consisted of a mass of laid brickwork
> rising up to a height of approximately 50 centimeters above the Early Dynastic
> ground surface. They were therefore relatively low in height, but enormously
> long: the shortest was about 19 meters long, the longest 29 meters. The average
> length of all twelve was about 27.40 meters (89 and 1/2 feet). . . . Each grave had
> originally been thickly coated with mud plaster and whitewash, so the impres-
> sion would have been of twelve (or more) huge white "boats" moored out in the
> desert, gleaming brilliantly in the Egyptian sun. (O'Connor 1991: 11)

These were not *burials*, but boats sunk into the Netherworld meant to be
sailing through it, to the world of chaos beyond the borders. They were still
followed by the "king" smiting the Westerners, as seen on the ivory label of
Den. Instead of the "king" flying through the Gate of Horus, boats were now
buried along the outer perimeter of the enclosure to make the journey to the
chaotic land beyond the border bringing the prestige goods home through the
Netherworld.

Here the "king's" *ka* would be in command, smiting the Westerners lending further evidence to understanding the "white crown" as a *ka*-sign at this

early stage in Ancient Egyptian development. Enclosures were accordingly dedicated to Khenti-Amentiu, "Foremost of the Westerners."

Building these new enclosures, seem to be a kind of formalization of tax collection, now having the different provinces come sailing with their tribute in the name of local gods. Exchange thereby appeared as taking place between gods, who were sanctioning the position of the "king."

When the processions from the provinces arrived by the Nile and anchored in front of the enclosures lead by their "god," their *bas* having taken possession of their "symbols" the first thing they saw was that the *ka*-boats from the Netherworld had already arrived, probably with their cargo to be exchanged for the products they carried to the enclosures.

Being the gathering point for The Followers of Horus, these enclosures also house the *sed*. Within the enclosure at Hierakonpolis, built by Khasekhemwy, there were found a relief composition made of pink granite in which the "king" is depicted wearing the sign of *ka* and there is also depicted a kiosk. Both are telling us that enclosures were also the place for the *sed*-festival (Wengrow 2009: 248).

Sed is often seen as a celebration of the united "Kingdom." Therefore the two daises shown on "pictures" of the festival are interpreted as "thrones" for the king on which he sits wearing the "crowns" of Upper and Lower Egypt respectively. To show the unity of the two lands, and that the "king" commands both, he is then believed to run along the perimeter of the court, taking the two lands in his possession.

The standard narrative of the *sed* goes something like this:

> It is believed that the ceremonies represented a ritual reenactment of the unification of Egypt, traditionally accomplished by Menes. From numerous wall reliefs and paintings and from the Heb-Sed court in the Step Pyramid complex of Djoser, in Saqqarah, much information has been gleaned about the festival. The king first presented offerings to a series of gods and then was crowned, first with the white crown of Upper Egypt and then with the red crown of Lower. Finally, the king, dressed in a short kilt with an animal's tail in back, ran a ritual course four times and was then carried away in a great procession to visit the chapels of the gods of Upper and Lower Egypt. (Encyclopædia Britannica 2018)

Then comes the conundrum. All the "rituals" performed in relationship to the *sed* are believed by many to have altered between the "king" representing Upper and Lower Egypt wearing the red and white crown befitting the occasions. As Frankfort describes the thrones involved in the "ritual":

> The throne of the king is in reality one of a pair. In the hieroglyph of the *Sed* festival (the hieroglyph) the two thrones appear, empty, in two pavilions placed back to back.

Then it goes completely wrong:

> This may be merely a graphic way of combining the two royal seats, which in
> reality stood side by side The dual pavilions allows Pharaoh to appear as king of
> Upper or of Lower Egypt according to the requirements of the ritual. (Frankfort
> 2000 [1948]: 85)

For Frankfort, the Egyptians were obviously tinkering with their representation to circumvent an artistic problem, instead of showing what Frankfort
would have liked to see. These difficulties of understanding the *sed*, all arises
because of the assumption that the uniting of Upper and Lower Egypt was
the all-important event in Egyptian History. Everything after this assumed
event must therefore necessarily reflect it. Also the *sed*. But if unification
was a gradual process, there would be no episode to enact "ritually" and if
the "crowns" were not expression of Upper and Lower Egypt, the *sed* practice
must be about something else.

From Djorser's pyramid complex, we can gather that the inside of all the
enclosures were lined with shines, probably for the different "Followers of
Horus," who on arrival might have placed their god inside these, advertising
their presence by their standards and flags. Thereby, the "gods" enlightened
in the shines making them come "alive."

At the enclosures there were boats arriving by the Nile and some other
boats was anchored underground, "buried" in the Netherworld. Consequently, we immediately recognize that all these enclosures were meant as
meeting points for the two realms of existence, and thereby deserving the
term "architecture for the next world."

By the "smiting" scenes, is seems that the "kings" *ka* were associated with
foreign lands and precious objects, sailing into the chaos beyond Egypt's borders. This ability expresses his power, being able to act with the gods whose
substance were made of gold. Hathor's presence on Narmer's Palette seems
to express the same idea.

We may therefore surmise that the *sed*, taking place in this environment,
contemplated the same cosmological duality. Takin place in front of "The
Followers of Horus," the "king" appeared alternately as Horus and as Khenti-
Amentiu (his own *ka*) thereby demonstrating his command of both realm, and
confirming his position as the protector of the people. He also demonstrated
this by encircling the two realms.

We find this depicted, for instance, in the subterranean panels in Djoser's
pyramid, where he is carrying two objects as he performs "the circuit of the
Two Lands" (Wengrow 2006: 230). During the proceedings the "king moves
around in a great loom to integrate the different aspect of cosmos, in a process that is called 'assuming the protection of the two lands" (Frankfort 2000

[1948]: 85). After this demonstration of power, the "king" had confirmed his position as sole proprietor of the two lands/realms of existence.

Enclosures complemented sumptuous graves in showing the status of the "king." They were a development in the status of the "king" as ruler of the two realms of cosmos and at the same time they were a more formalized way of collecting taxes, which the Ancient Egyptians seems to have envisaged as an exchange between "gods."

These "gods" came sailing to the enclosures from the different provinces with their product. Arriving at the enclosure, they were met with the sight of already moored underground boats sailing in from the Netherworld and connecting the "king to the Westerners." This is probably the reason for entitling Khasekhemwy "Chief of the Westerners," envisaged as his ability to "smite" he Westerners.

These enclosures as being "The Fortress of the Gods," connected the two realms/lands of cosmos. Being able to do this was seen as the base for the power of the "king," who thereby provided sustenance for his people and especially for his court. It was therefore also the place for the enactment of the *sed*. In this event, the "king" opened the gates between the two realms, being alternatively his own *ka* (in the Netherworld—Khenti-Amentiu) and *ba* (in Light Land—Horus). This enactment of being able to act in the two realms alternatively showed his immense power and his ability to provide "life-force" to the communities.

THE PYRAMID

Pyramids have been submitted to some peculiar interpretations, landing devises for space ships, giant fertilizers, power plants, shines for holy scripts, the list is endless. Apart from these, there are also some obvious problems with standard interpretations of pyramids being graves and nothing else. Most of the pyramids are constructed in a way that would make any normal funeral almost impossible, the location of the entrance sometimes high above ground level, the passageway to the burial chamber makes it almost impossible to bring a coffin into the burial room, and there are rooms without any obvious purposes.

It is not until Unas's pyramid from the Fifth Dynasty that we get a better understanding of what is going on inside these massive constructions, because its rooms are covered with hieroglyphs, presumably telling the story about its purpose, although this may have changed in the cause of history.

Even the first pyramid built by Djoser is an enigma. The main problem is that the granite burial vault in the main step pyramid is much too small to have facilitated an actual burial (Ancient Egypt—History 2016). There are also another structure called the South Tomb, that has a similar burial vault as in the main pyramid, but it is even smaller, certainly too small for a human burial (Lehner 1997: 92).

To complicate matters, there is only one real entrance to the complex (and many so-called dummy entrances). The "real" entrance leads to a narrow passageway that connects to a roofed colonnade. This means that Djoser's funeral cortege would have had to negotiate an elaborate course through the building, where many of the passages are scarcely widen than 1meter (Lehner 1997: 85). Not an optional entrance for the splendid funeral possession we imagine surrounded the dead king when it entered the complex and proceeded to place the corps in the burial chamber.

Lehner have a somewhat ingenious solution to the problem of getting the corpse of the dead king into the compound without using the doorway and thereby compensate for the architect Imhotep's failures. He thinks that instead of using the narrow door,

> it would have been far more convenient to bring the royal body and its accoutrements into the complex by way of a ramp over the enclosure in its northeast corner. (Lehner 1997: 85)

This seems unnecessary extra work, if all it took was to build a proper entrance that allowed for the assumed procession. After all, it could not have come as a surprise that they had to get the corpse into the compound, and further on to the burial chamber.

Next came Sekhemkeht. His pyramid is a special case. It is called the Buried Pyramid, and the unfinished pyramid. It only reached 8 meters (26 feet), and the interior was left unfinished (The Mystery of Sekhemkhet's Pyramid 2016). In The Turin Papyrus this king is only given a reign of six years (Lehner 1997: 94).

A native Egyptologist, Zakaria Goneim, while excavating a pile of rubble next to Djoser's pyramid, discovered it in 1954 (The Mystery of Sekhemkhet's Pyramid 2016). It was undisturbed. During the excavation, the team found hundreds of stone vessels of many kinds, 120 storage magazines, and a gold jewelry treasure believed to have been kept in a wooden chest. These finds made Goneim write, they "provided us with a valuable clue to the fact that, in spite of its unfinished state, *the pyramid had been used for burial*" (The Mystery of Sekhemkhet's Pyramid 2016).

After months of hard excavation work under which one person died, they finally entered the burial chamber where they found a sarcophagus carved from a single alabaster block that had a sliding panel opening at one end. It was sealed and untouched. This was the first time ever that an unopened sarcophagus was found in a pyramid. This was to be Tutankhamun all over again. Finally, the sarcophagus was opened in the presence of a vast number of journalists. The panel was lifted and they all stared into an empty sarcophagus. Some called it "Pharaoh Fiasco." Goneim was later falsely accused for stealing antiquities and ended up drowning himself in the Nile in 1957 (The Mystery of Sekhemkhet's Pyramid 2016).

Jean-Phillipe Lauer took over the excavation of the Sekhemkhet site in 1963. In his opinion, the mummy of Sekhemkhet, along with the burial goods, had been removed during the First Intermediate Period, a time when he thinks that many of the other Old Kingdom pyramids were plundered (The Mystery of Sekhemkhet's Pyramid 2016). However, this does not explain the gold treasure and the sealed sarcophagus.

You cannot blame the architect for the premature death of the king, but you would want to know why he sealed an empty sarcophagus during the construction phase, and why the other officials did not insists on bury the king in it.

What we *do* see, is an example of pyramid work in progress, showing the stages involved. It seems that the underground structure was completed in outline with galleries and "burial" chamber, and to all intent with a sealed sarcophagus, before the top structure and the rest of the complex was finished. No matter if, the king was alive or dead.

There were some more abandoned attempts to build pyramids before we get to the Maidum pyramid finished by Sneferu. Here there are no sarcophagus and no trace of one has been found; only a corbelled room that seem to have been deemed sufficient. Maybe they forgot about the sarcophagus, but if so, it would have been very complicated to get one into the burial chamber. At the Maidum pyramid, the entrance is 30 m up the side of the pyramid, from where there is a *descending* passage for 58 m that is 0.85 m wide and 1.65 m high, ending in a horizontal passage. From there, there was a vertical shaft leading 16.6 m up into the burial chamber just above the first step (Lehner 1997: 98).

Such complicated and narrow entrances are typical for all pyramids. If these structures were ever meant to be used as burial places, the architects went to great effort to complicate the placement of the dead inside them. The funeral cortege must have hated the constructors. Moreover, this unhappy scenario would continue for centuries. If they constructed the interior of the pyramids to be so complicated to access to avoid tomb robberies, as is the current view, you would thing that a thousand years later, they would have found out that it did not work—or something else was at play.

If the internal structures of pyramids were means to protect against grave robbers, the Egyptians must have had this on their minds from the construction of the first pyramid (premonitions of grave robbers). It is however rather odd that they continued with the same internal design for nearly 500 years, given that they must have acknowledged that it did not prevent grave robbers.

Still they seem to have happily continued building the same structure. So maybe the internal design is not to prevent grave robbers. They knew how to prevent grave robbers, which Khufu showed when burring his wife: in an unmarked, deep horizontal shafts filled with rubble.

These early pyramids remain majestically silent about their purpose and function. Enigmas for all posterity. If they were so good at building large structures with precision, why could they not construct a proper entrance, one that could easily accommodate the funeral possession—and which could still be secured from grave robbers? There is also the possibility that we do not see what they saw, that our logic is different from theirs. Fortunately, the situation changed with the last king of the Fifth Dynasty. That is still a long way away from the first pyramid.

We need a cosmological explanation of pyramids. Therefore, we have to start with the first of its kind. Djoser's pyramid. In a way, he started out following the example of his father Khasekhemwy who built one of the largest enclosures. He was buried in Abydos. Before Khasekhemwy, Egypt had gone through at long time of recession (called the Second Dynasty) losing its connection to the Westerners, and there were built no enclosures (maybe the "gods" had left).

At Khasekhemwy time things had changed and Egypt was back on track, even richer than before. So Khasekhemwy was named "Overseer of Foreign Lands" (Tyldesley 2003: 81–82). Despite his status, he was buried as a mortal, as a human being, in a *mastaba*, as all other "kings" before him.

Maybe to illustrate Egypt's sudden leap in wealth, Djoser decided to build a replica of his father's enclosure in stone. We must therefore assume that it was built with the same purpose as earlier enclosures, collecting tax, staging the *sed*, and so on.

By another bold move, he placed his *mastaba* on the same place where his father had built a mound. It was constructed like ordinary *mastabas* but with the most elaborate and huge storage facilities underground ever seen. By this move, he appropriated "The Fortress of the Gods." He placed himself in the middle of all the shrines for the "gods" of all the provinces. He was surely mingling with the gods.

Something, an event, a dream or just out of being megalomaniac, convinced Djoser that this was not enough. In successive stages, he turned his *mastaba* into a mound (in the shape of a mountain). This time completely in stone (Tyldesley 2003: 88–90). As Arnold notices, this move signaled "different ideas about the royal afterlife" (Arnold 1997: 42). For this change to take place, a similar re-conceptualization must have taken place in the understanding of the living royal person. Djoser must have changed status from being a mere mortal as his father to become a living "god."

To be sure, the construction of pyramids was a new development in Ancient royalty. Going from graves, to enclosures to pyramids. Djoser's pyramid represent the first major shift in Ancient cosmology. At this point, the "king" was transformed from a human being with special abilities to become a living "god," not an easy transformation.

Regardless of their statuses and abilities, sumptuous graves and enclosures, the previous "kings" were buried as human beings. All the former rulers were mortals. Their graves testify to this. They had special abilities to contact and act in the Netherworld and these were played out in the enclosures. Not so with Djoser. By combining the enclosure with his *mastaba*, Djoser placed himself among the "gods." He was no longer a "manifestation" of the sky god Horus. He had by placing his final resting place in the "Fortress of the Gods" elevate his status to being a "god." Being a "god" a *mastaba* must have seemed inappropriate.

This shift and the building of a pyramid was not just to provide eternal life for the king amongst the stars. It involved a complete rethinking of the "king's" existence and therefore also of cosmology. It is not possible to bury a "god." This would be against the normal conception of "gods" as beings existing in the unseen realm of cosmos. From this realm, they visited and intervened in the life of the living. Their *bas* took up residence in different objects from where they were supposed to act, and bring life to the scenarios depicted. It is not an easy matter to reverse this train of event and put a human being into the world of non-corporal beings.

Building a huge Primordial Mound in the form of a pyramid and bury the "king" in it, will not in itself do the trick and transform the "king" into a "god." Maybe decades of intermingling with the "gods" and acting in both realms made Djoser think that he himself had become a "god." We do not know what caused it—maybe just excessive wealth.

Redefining Djoser as a "god" would immediately pose problems. "Gods" and human are constituted differently, and have their "home" in different realms of cosmos. This is the result of bringing death into existence, and thereby everlasting life for gods (*djet*) and passing existence for humans (*neheh*). The differently constitution of "gods" and humans were reflected in the behavior of their *bas*. "God's" *bas* descended from the Netherworld/ Heaven on some form of "images," while human's *bas* visited the realm of "gods" during sleep. Djoser could not be both!

Building a pyramid does not solve this problem. It seems that these issues were not quite clarified at this time, since Djoser and his successors both had graves and mounds. It seems that the Egyptians had not yet decided if their "king" was going to be buried as a human, or if he was going to live as a "god" in the Netherworld inside the mound.

To solve the dilemma, Horus (now in the form of Djoser) could have been redefined as being the *ba* of Khenti-Amentiu (Chief of the Westerners/Netherworld), and the "king's" body being a vehicle for this *ba*, as a living Horus. Whereby the "king" and his body would merely act as a passing "container" for this *ba*, his body being endlessly interchangeable with the bodies of coming "king's," like statues in "temples."

The "king's" bodies would then have had to be re-conceptualized as a fleeting and temporarily habitat for the *ba* of Khenti-Amentiu. To be a true "god" the "king" could not have a (human) body! The coffin, or what has been called the sarcophagus, would then forever be the homestay of Khenti-Amentiu (later substituted with Osiris). Djoser, as a "god" did not have to be buried (you cannot bury a "god"! Then the "God" would suddenly have a corpse in the Netherland, which could not happen).

The whereabouts of the "king's" (human) corpse is probably reflected, or explored later, in the narrative about Osiris. He is "killed" and dismembered, thrown into the Nile, found by Isis, and reassembled in the coffin in the Netherworld of the pyramid. Maybe this is the fate of all "kings." The "king's" body/corpse was not important. It was always replaceable. This is why the "king" could have a body but not a (physically) corpse.

As David writes, "no burial has ever been discovered inside a pyramid" (2002: 96), and the pyramid "temples" were "not used for the royal funerary procession" (David 2002: 104). It might also explain all the sealed but empty sarcophaguses. So the story about the murder of Osiris is not a "myth," but a manual for the fate of any pharaoh. Explained repeatedly in all the pyramids with hieroglyphs.

By the time of Sneferu, the ideology of a divine "king" seem to have been more fully implemented. At this time the strange undecidedness of the "king's" status expressed in the double nature of the Step Pyramid being both a grave and a mound subsided. This duality in the construction of pyramids were given up. From now on, the status of the "king" seem to have been firmly defined. It was no longer necessary to have an underground grave with storage rooms. The "king's" *ba* could leave the pyramid at will and embody in one of the many statues erected for him, and his provisions could be brought to him at the statues.

One of the changes showing the conceptual clarification about the "king's" status is that the grave was abandoned, and that there appears a tiny cultic area in front of the east side of the pyramid. It is the first time that a "cultic" installation is directly connected to a royal tomb; "no altars or offering places have been found in any of the earlier funerary complexes" (Arnold 1997: 45). Before, the "king" had to rely on his underground storerooms. Now the King could come out from the pyramid and consume the *bas* of all the "offerings," while the humans could dispose of the *kas* of these (also issues known from contemporary kinship based societies).

Now the "king's" full divinity was realized. Gone are the inconsistencies. It is now realized that the dead "king's" *ba* could come out through the thick walls and receive their offerings. No need to store them. Another significant change was that the whole pyramid complex was rotated ninety degrees, so that it was oriented east-west rather than north-south, indicating that the sun had become one of the major gods connected to the pyramids (Arnold 1997: 45).

This seems to have continued throughout the remainder of the pyramid era. Decades later, we find the same principles regarding the pyramid and the *ba*. As late as in the Fifth Dynasty, Sahure's pyramid was named "The Rising of the Ba spirit," and his brother's, who succeeded him, was called "Kakai [Neferirkare] is a soul [*ba*]" (Tyldesley 2003: 180).

By now the cosmic principle were in place, delineating the roles of "gods" and "kings." However, the personal could be substituted. Later and probably for political reasons, and surely by the time of Khufu, the "gods" of Djoser were substituted with other "gods." Re and Osiris were by this time the major protagonists in the cosmic order of the "kings." Osiris being "buried" in the pyramid. Re traveling through the pyramid at night. Horus, the "king" being the *ba* of Osiris. Their relationship was now part of "genesis" and the cosmic order.

By this time, the pyramids were moved away from the Nile. They (probably) still served as nodes for tax/tribute collection (although in a more formalized way), having ships coming in with their cargoes, to exchange these for the product brought in by the *ka*-boats sunk around the pyramids, and probably partly visible for the visitors. Being away from the Nile, they needed an anchorage point and an unloading place, called a "Valley Temple." From here they had to approach the pyramid through a long corridor a passage into the *ka*-world of the pyramid, called a "Passageway," only to emerge in front of the "god" in the form of a statue, or several statues, that were the master of the following exchange, called the "Offering Temple." As we know from the Ancient cosmology and conception of personhood these were not mere statues, they were the "god."

To be married to a "god" probably meant that the wife(s) were also considered divine (and sometime they were kins), or there would have been a miss-match. These wives would therefore have had their own pyramids, and being the *ba* of some female goddesses (which never have been disclosed), providing female pyramids around the major male pyramids. These female pyramids would represent the matrilineal part of the "kings" power.

By the end of the Fifth Dynasty the layout of the pyramid had found a final form, but probably only refining the principles of all the pyramids since Sneferu. There are certain changes along the way, especially in the number of chambers and internal corridors. At this time, the pyramids are suddenly equipped with manuals, telling to what is going on inside them. From Unas onwards, the inside of the chambers and corridors are covered with long hieroglyphic texts, called "The Pyramid Texts."

These texts were discovered in 1880 and have subsequently been found in the tombs of eleven "kings" and "queens" pyramids at Saqqara. Kurth Sethe prepared a concordance of these texts, which appeared in 1908 (Allen 2015: 2). This did nothing to further our general understanding of Egyptian cosmology or to the purpose of pyramids in particular.

In Sethes's rendering the texts appeared as a strange mixture of fragmentary "religious" texts. This was due to the way Sethe presented the texts. He misunderstood the sequence of the texts, and therefore they were presented in some kind of artificial order. This way of presenting the texts concealed both the sequentiality of each corpus of the texts and the relationship between the texts and the wall on which they were inscribed (Allan 2015: 2).

Since Jean Leclant and his work on the Pyramid Texts, it has become clear that the texts are ordered by rooms, walls, and columns, rather than sequentially around the pyramids (Allan 1994: 5). Sethe did not recognize the role played by the physical location in the choice of meaning of each text in the pyramid (Allan 1994: 5). According to Allan, it is possible to read from the content and location of these groups of texts, the purpose of each element in the burial complex itself (Allan 1994: 7).

There is a sequence to the episodes taking place inside the pyramid, which are ordered according to their position in the different rooms. In the so-called burial chamber there are what Allan terms "Offering Rituals" consisting of liberation, water and incense, mouth opening, small meal, oil, eye paint, clothing. This is for instance seen in the text:

> Osiris Unis, take the Eye of Horus: lift it up for yourself to your face. Lifting up the bread and beer. (Allan 1994: 12)

A big meal and the smashing of the vessels used close this part of the "collecting" of tribute/tax/offerings. This is followed by a set of "Utterances" on the southern half of the "burial chamber," where the "dead king" is identified with Osiris (proving that inside all appearances of king in the human world there were the same substance):

> (Osiris) your body is the body of this Unis, your flesh is the flesh of this Unis, your bones are this Uni's bones. (Allan 1994: 15)

Unis (Unas) is then urged to travel along with Re in his daily cycle:

> Go after your sun . . . and be beside the god, and leave your house to your son of your begetting.

Re Atum, this Unis has come to you. . . . You two shall travel the above together from the dusk; you two shall rise from the Akhet, where you have become *akh*.

Oh Unis, you have not gone away dead; you have gone away alive. (Allan 1994: 15–16)

These two sequences, by Allan called the "Offering Ritual" and "Resurrection Ritual" (collecting tribute and connecting with Re) constitutes nearly all the "Utterances" in the burial chamber and passage.

In the so-called antechamber the scenes changes. First, the "dead king" praises, or are told who provided the "offerings," which was evidently performed or led by his successor, Horus:

Your son Horus has acted for you. (Allan 1994: 18)

In the "antechamber," the king emerges from the Duat/Netherworld, and ends with him demanding entrance to "the gateway of Nu." In between, the text is mainly concerned with the "dead kings" (Osiris) progress in and through various regions of the pre-dawn sky, and ends with a text that is primarily concerned with his ascent to the sky (Allan 1994: 19). The "king" is leaving the pyramid as a *ba*:

My face is that of falcons, my wings are those of birds . . . . I have used my arms as a goose, I have beat my wings as a kite. Someone has flown away, men: I have flown away from you. (Allan 1994: 19)

He then demands to be let out:

Draw the "Baboon's penis" (= the doorbolt)! Open the door of the sky! (Allan 1994: 20)

This door to be opened is probably what is generally called a portcullis (thought to have preventive means from introducers). Instead, it is the door to heaven.

Then the "king" participates in the sunrise, and "he clears away the night . . . sends away the night hours" and demand transportation from the ferryman:

So that I may go out it to the sky and attend the sun in the sky. (Allan 1994: 20)

He has however to traverse the night sky before his uniting with the sun at dawn. Night is equivalent to the conditions of the universe before the moment of creation, and the chaos of the primeval ocean, Nu. He is now standing at the gateway of Nu, ready to merge into the waters of the pre-creation/pre-sunrise universe (Allan 1994: 22).

To connect this travel to the rooms and wall we have to link the story to the larger cosmology. Having a "god" as king means that he is part of the cosmic cyclical regeneration based on Atum, Re, Nut, and so on. Nut was not only the goddess of the sky and the surface that Re traveled across by day, she was also Re's mother. He was thought to gestate at night within her womb, and to be born at dawn. This happened during his travel in the Night boat sailing through the Duat/Netherworld. During this voyage, he united with Osiris as *ba* and *ka* respectively.

Hereafter Re proceeded through the Akhet, the eastern part of the horizon a zone just before sunrise. Here Re became capable of an independent life. On the other hand, Osiris were thought to inhabit both the womb of Nut, where he met with Re, and the Duat where he was "king." Within the womb, he embodied the force that gave Re new life to appear at dawn, and he was himself reborn in his son Horus (Allan 2015: 9–10).

The layout of the inside of the pyramid is therefore not just some otherwise, haphazardly, connected and empty rooms. To make it possible for the "king" to accomplish this journey, the internal architecture of the pyramids mimic the "cosmos." Hence, the layout of the internal structure reflects or are based on Ancient cosmology. It could not be otherwise. This is the guiding line behind all Egyptian practices.

Inside the pyramid the different aspect of travelling through the Duat, meeting with Re, continue through the Akhet and then raise toward the sky is reflected in the lay out of the rooms, their relation to each other and to the texts inscribed on their walls. At night, the deceased passed through these rooms and corridors.

Under the apex of the pyramid lies the so-called burial chamber with the so-called sarcophagus. In reality, this chamber is the Duat, and the box inside it is Nut's womb. These walls are inscribed with texts that urge the deceased to (re)enter Nut's womb. Other texts are about how the dead "king" (now Osiris) can be released from the body and begin his journey towards dawn. The deceased "king" is always addressed as Osiris, for example, "Osiris Unis" (Allan 2015: 11).

After having been released from Osiris's body the "king's" *ba* travels to the so-called antechamber, which is the Akhet, from where he is supposed to join up with Re who have by now become an independent being, and so the relationship between Osiris and Re as *ka* an *ba* in the womb of Nut is for the time suspended. Thus to be able to participate in the onward journey Osiris must be his own *akh* (*ba*), leaving his inert *ka* behind whose *ba* is now in Horus.

The so-called *serdab* room to the east of the Akhet (antechamber) is the eastern limit of the Akhet and it is the point at which Re and the deceased left the womb of Nut to proceed through her birth canal—the corridor. Then they proceed towards the sky through the corridor, vestibule and ascending corridor, crossing from the Akhet toward the sky. Between the "corridor" and the "vestibule," there are what has mistakenly been called portcullis, which must be the gates, which Re and Osiris must open and proceed through into the sky:

> The double doors of heaven are open for thee; the double doors of . . . are undone for thee, "Greetings," says Isis; "ferry on in peace," says Nephthys's. Utterance 553. (Mercer 2008: 317)

Pyramids are then *cosmic perpetuating devises*. Without them, existence would grind to a halt. They sustained the order of society and the king's position and his role in upholding this order, which the Egyptians called Maat.

As places that connect "gods" and regenerates cosmos, it only seems appropriate that the living "king's" *sed* were conducted within these perimeters. He then demonstrated his affinity with both Osiris and Re, being a son of the former, and therefore connected to their cyclical regeneration of cosmos.

To house this formidable event it had to take place in the primordial mound, and it had to be built to withstand the forces unleashed, a rock solid construction. It was the primordial mound as a mountain, the way the primordial mound was possible conceived in the first place.

We must assume that all previous pyramid also grabbled with these issues and how the "king" was related to the ancestral world and the role that the pyramid laid in regenerating his power and cosmos at the same time. There are surely differences in how these issues were incorporated in the design of the pyramid, but they must all essentially have been about such issues about cosmos and the "king." Maybe the descending corridor in Khufu's Pyramid leading into an underground chamber is simply an access way for Re to enter the Duat and Nut's womb in the pyramid to link up with Osiris in the "Kind's Chamber."

The Pyramid texts are not at all concerned with the burial of the "dead king" and his funeral procession into the burial chamber. These texts are wholly concerned with the "king" receiving "offerings," and how he meet up with Re as a *ba*, to participate in his travel in the day-boat, that is, how he is leaving the pyramid. *Going Forth by Day*.

This means that the entrances to the pyramids are not entrances. They are exit-doors. Accordingly the descending corridor is actually and ascending corridor, leading the *ba* upward to the sky. This might help explain the curious positions of these "entrances," often high above ground level, making funerals next to impossible.

As a logical extension of this, there is after all no mentioning of "resurrection" in the Pyramid Texts. Such an issue is not part of Ancient cosmology. It is all about how the *bas* relate to humans and gods. Accordingly, we are not told about any corpse in the Texts, only that Unis (or any other dead "king") is now Osiris. A new Osiris to be sure but eternally the same. As we know, Isis assembles Osiris in the Netherworld after his brother Set dismembered him. Like all the rest of the "gods," Osiris therefore does not possess an earthly body.

Likewise, "kings" cannot leave earthly corpses that can be buried literally. Cosmology and Ancient concept of personhood dictates that if the "kings" were a mere mortal he would need his corpse for his *ba* to reside in. If on the other hand, his was a "god," he cannot have a corpse. This is just to say that according to Ancient cosmology, the dead "king" always merges into Osiris. How the Ancient managed this problem is presently unknown but we know that all the dead "kings," who were to become Osiris, were all assembled by Isis—again and again—in the non-corporal Netherworld.

Maybe the fate of dead "kings" resembles Osiris's fate after being killed by Set. Otherwise, it would refute the status of Osiris, as "god" According to Ancient cosmology, we can only "meet" the *ba* of the "gods" that descend and enlighten their man-made images. Therefore, we are told in the Pyramid Texts about the endeavors of the deceased "king's" *ba*. The Ancients, could not suddenly have a physically Osiris in the form of the deceased "king." This would be matter out of place.

In this way, pyramids cannot be seen as burial places of megalomaniac pharaohs. No burial in a Western way ever took place inside these constructions. Therefore, we find sealed sarcophagus in unfinished pyramid. Real physically (Western) corpse was never meant to be placed in these. Isis did the work.

This is only half the story about pyramids. Attached to their outside there was a delivery construction (called an offering temple). Pyramids all stood within large enclosures (called pyramid complexes), and they were connected by long corridors (called causeways) leading to the river Nile where there was a reception housing (called a valley temple).

While the inside of the pyramids were dedicated to exiting the Duat, the outside was dedicated on how to get provision into the pyramids, that is, going into the Duat. It therefore seems likely that the outside was an inverse version of the inside. In the inside, we have a movement from Nut's womb (the sarcophagus), in the Duat (burial chamber), to the Akhet (antechamber) to the day-sky (corridor).

On the outside there was a movement from the "valley temple" through a corridor, to the "offering temple" (attached to the Pyramid) where the "offerings" were placed in front of statues of the "king" (as the embodiment of the "king's" *ba* and thus a living entity). "Offering" processions were moving towards the Duat, but was stopped short just in front of it since humans cannot enter the Duat while alive. Here they handed over their "offerings" (tax/ tribute) to the awaiting "king." These provision's *bas* were then transported into the Duat/burial chamber. Provisions that were essential for Osiris (NN) to be able to be *Going forth by Day.*

Since we have no descriptions of these outside installations, we do not know what the Ancient called them. Maybe the valley temple was equivalent to the Akhet when traveling the other way, the causeway would then be the night sky, the offering temple the entrance to the Duat with Nut and Osiris inside prepared to receive the "offerings." Until further finds, we cannot know.

Building pyramids had nothing to do with megalomaniac "kings." It is also clear that the Ancient could not refrain from building them. If they did, the sun would never raise and shine again. Life would grind to a halt. However, this cosmology had to be severely reinterpreted during the "First Intermediate Period," when "kings" lost their status. After this there were to be no more pyramids.

THE COSMOS

Ancient cosmology is essential for understanding Ancient practices and their iconography. From the *Papyrus of Ani* (one version of *Going Forth by Day*), we find one of the most iconic images from Ancient Egypt. It is tucked in between two scene showing Ani and his wife Tutu in the beginning of the papyrus. In both of these initials scenes, they appear as living persons, dressed to participate in some formal occasion. But from the accompanying text to the first scene, Ani is given the epithets "the Osiris" and "vindicated" and he is therefore undisputable deceased and acting in the invisible realm of existence.

In the first scene, the couple stand before two offering stands while the text is dedicated to Re. In the next scene, they are again standing in front of two offering tables this time offering to Osiris (Goelet 2015: 164). In the text to the first scene Re is greeted:

He says, Hail to you, you having come as Khepri, even Khepri who is the creator of the gods. (Faulkner and Goelet 2015: Plate 1-A)

In the next scene, Osiris is hailed:

Worship of Osiris Wennefer, the great God who dwells in the Thinite nome, King of Eternity, Lord of Everlasting, who passes millions of years in his lifetime. (Faulkner and Goelet 2015: Plate 2-A)

It seems that the two scenes with the deceased Ani is dedicated to the *neheh* and *djet*, aspects of his being in the Afterlife, referred to by the presence of Re and Osiris, respectively, the two major "gods" of the Afterlife. In between these two scenes, we have a scene without caption or text. This "chapter was never accompanied by text" (Faulkner and Goelet 2015: 164). It is just there. The whole composition of the scene looks very much like a statement, a tableau.

Goelet gives a basic description of the scene. Let us just start with this formal description. Goelet notice that on top of the "picture" there is an elongated arch forming the sign *pet* for sky. Directly beneath it, he observes the sign for "life," the *ankh*, equipped with two arms lifting up the sun disc (Re). According to Goelet the *ankh* stands upon a *djet* pillar (Osiris—it has eye) flanked by Isis and Nephthys who are recognizable only by their headgear. Both are sitting on a hieroglyph for gold, *nub*, which are placed on a mat that in turn is placed on the sign for "mountain," *dju* (Faulkner and Goelet 2015: 164).

Because of the presence of Osiris-Re who are split into two deities, he thinks that the whole

scene illustrates the beginning of the sun's daily journey through the sky, when it emerges out of the desert horizon after its nighttime journey underneath the earth and through the Duat. (Faulkner and Goelet 2015: 164)

It could as well illustrate the meeting of Osiris and Re in the Netherworld acting to rejuvenate the cosmos. All the elements are there, the assembled Osiris by his sisters and Shu with raised hands in the *ka*-gesture raising up Re toward the sky. However, neither of these interpretations addresses the presence of the *ankh*, the sign for life, perched in between Osiris and Re.

Let us look at the basic description as reflecting Ancient cosmology. Directly beneath the "sky," which is Nut, is Re who are lifted up by two upraised arms in the *ka*-stance, which is Shu. This seems connected to the *ankh*, the sign for life, which is equipped with its usual cross bar that has nothing to do with the arms lifting Re (then the *ankh* would have both arms and crossbar). It connects to a *djed* pillar, which is Osiris with Re, and it is flanked by Osiris's two sisters Isis and Nephthys, who are both sitting on the hieroglyphic sign for gold, *nub*. These are placed on the sign for mountain, which must be Geb. The whole tableau seems to depict *Ma'at* or Tefnut.

Everything is in place, and the right relationship between "deities" established. So in this tableau, we are presented with all the major figures concerning "genesis" and the introduction of death. Life as it unfolds between "gods," among whom Ani is now going to live.

Curiously, the two sisters are sitting on a foundation of gold. Since you cannot "draw" gold, they are sitting on the hieroglyph for gold. But since the "symbol" is the thing, they are sitting on gold. In turn, they are sitting on the hieroglyphic sign for "mountain," which according to the same cultural logic means that they are *ipso facto* sitting on a mountain. First, it "proves" that "gods" and gold were interchangeable. Second, it must be the final proof that the primeval mound was indeed a mountain, a mountain of gold—gold being the ultimate source of prestige in Upper Egypt all through the ages.

Only, the *ankh* seems matter out of place. The way the *ankh* is generally described immediately sets us on the wrong track.

It is a cross with a loop at the top sometimes ornamented with symbols or decorative flourishes but most often simply a plain gold cross. (Mark 2018a)

Such a definition is purely in the eye of the beholder. It leads one to think about Christian symbolism in which the cross has a significant place. There is no cross! Then the "stick" would have had to continue across the bar. Instead, there is a "circle." At the most, we see a T-shaped structure with a circle on top.

This "sign" has had many fanciful interpretations over the years. One that is repeatedly stated is taken from Alan H. Gardiner, who claimed that the *ankh* represents a sandal strap. He thought so because the sandal was a daily part of an Egyptian's life and the *ankh* symbol therefore came to symbolize life (Mark 2018b).

E. A. Wallis Budge, claimed the *ankh* originated from the belt buckle of the goddess Isis and he therefore thought it to be a ceremonial girdle representing the female genitalia and thus symbolizing fertility. The *ankh's* resemblance to this means that it is interpreted as a fertility symbol (Mark 2018b). More recently, Baines has, for some reason, suggested that the *ankh* represents a penis sheath (Pinch 2006: 110).

None of these interpretations is based on Ancient cosmology or culture, but only on the *ankh* having some superficial similarities with other mostly practical objects—but in Ancient Egypt the symbol was the devise, so these explanations completely misses Ancient cosmology.

To understand the *ankh*, we have to (re)insert it into Ancient cosmology and the concept of personhood. Here they had a concept for the invisible world called *djet* and a concept for the visible world called *neheh*—completeness and change. For them this was the whole of reality. It is for instance repeated in the relationship between Re and Osiris, and in the union between *ba* and corpse (*ka*).

This is what the *ankh* is all about: *djet* and *neheh*, "stick" (Osiris) and "circle" (Re). But they had to be held together to form a unity. In several depiction of this "object," Isis is appearing as a bird seemingly holding the two elements, the two lands, together. Simplified she is looking like a "cross-bar." Isis was also the one who mended Osiris after he had been killed. Thereby creating life after dead, and thus connected "the two lands" of the dead and the living. Isis connected the two realms that everybody was living in, *ba* and *ka*, as being *neheh* and *djet* (the two main categories in Ancient thought system).

What better ways to call these different aspects of being into "life" than by a "circle" that is endless; it goes round and round, no beginning and no end, as Re, and a "stick" that is complete; it remains the same. It might explain why Osiris is a pillar. This combination was "life" as the Ancient understood it. This is *ankh*; "Life." At any time, it could be enliven by the "gods."

It is now possible to "decipher" the "chapter" without text. It does not need any texts, the image is the message. It actually combines two "motives" or spheres of life. On one level, the "story" revolves around the major "gods," Osiris and Re, who in turn is flanked by most of the other "deities." This part clearly expresses the relationship between the two major categories among the "gods" in Ancient cosmology, the *djet* (Osiris) and *neheh* (Re). This is the basic relationship in Ancient cosmology and the one unraveled in the "story" about genesis.

But as we know this is only half the "story." Dead was introduced and cosmos from the on consisted of four interlinked categories, the one between "gods" in the invisible realm, and the same but reversed categories among the living in the visible realm. This last part could only be represented with the *ankh*—"life." So to represent the whole cosmos the *ankh* had to be there.

This double constellation is "cosmos." Therefore, this illustration stands alone. No words needed. This is cosmos. In all its simplicity, and in all its grandeur, brought to live by its iconography, it is the cosmos of Ani. What else do you need when you are dead? All, Ani needed to know was where he was. This is what the scene tells him. It lays out the whole cosmos in front of his eyes, ready to step into and making it possible for him to continue with his "life."

So one of the most iconic "pictures," from *Going Forth by Day* is calling the whole world into being for the diseased Ani (called The Ani Papyrus). Hereby, he had the whole world laid out in front of him, a world that would go on forever. It is there for the "gods" to enliven (just like statues), and make the world go around for Ani. Although it happened in his tomb.

To sum up, ancient practices from palettes, over enclosures and pyramids to iconography has to be understood as resulting from a specific Egyptian way of negotiating their life conditions. These were shaped by their position in a larger reproductive system that provided opportunities but also sat limits to the possible. Gold was essential in providing opportunities, but only for a small section of Egyptian society who became immensely rich. This situation was negotiated in stories about genesis which "explained" the cosmic order and the position of wealthy "kings" in it.

Therefore, cosmologies are closely linked to the reproductive conditions of societies, and together these shapes practice. By combining the reproductive conditions of Ancient Egypt and the cosmological order, we can provide new interpretations of otherwise heavily debated subject in Ancient Egypt.

The Narmer Palette is not about unification, but about the king, "illustrating" his position in the regional exchange network and his ability to act in both realms of existence, thereby providing prestige goods arriving from the Westerners beyond the border, whom Narmer is able to "smite."

Enclosures were not places for funerary preparations, but places for collecting tax and for the king to perform his abilities in providing these, illustrated by the "kings" *sed* in which he encircled the cosmos.

Pyramids are not graves, but places for the gods Re and Osiris to meet and rejuvenate each other in the womb of Nut who is the sarcophagus placed in the Duat, which is the burial chamber. Their meeting secured the continued existence of the known cosmos, and this meeting made it possible for the sun to raise and shine every new day. Osiris was always the dead "king," and Horus his son, was always substituted by another Horus also sired by the former Osiris (NN) to become the next Osiris. This happened in a continuously repetition.

This cosmos is shown in the papyri of Ani, in which we have all the gods in one realm superimposed with the *ankh*, sign of life, given the four cosmological categories of the Ancient, and providing eternal cosmos for Ani.

Conclusion

There are two complementary aspects necessary to understand the social evolution of Ancient Egypt, one international, the other Egyptian. Most studies only focusses on the last part. Then all social dynamic must be of local origin. Then Egypt's economic and social evolution must be related to internal affairs. Dynamic pharaohs, conquering pharaohs, tired pharaohs, palace revolutions, excessive bureaucracy, agricultural potential, and so on.

These assumptions has to be given up when Egypt is inserted in its regional context. Egypt's development was intimately connected to the Levant and Mesopotamia in the west, and to Nubia and beyond in the south. Both aspect has to be considered to understand the evolution of Ancient Egypt. As such, this study has incorporated these two aspects of social reproduction. It has been about regional conditions and local strategies seen as complementary aspects of social organization and local cosmology.

In this book, I have combined a kind of objectivist analysis of "real material" forces in the form of Egypt's interaction and trade with their neighbors, with a "subjectivist" analysis of the choices and strategies that the Egyptians employed in these circumstances. Egypt's position in a larger reproductive network created condition locally that the actors could not escape (because these conditions are based on a system that is larger than any of the local system that makes it up) but which also provided opportunities. Such regional systems also sets limits to the possible.

These local conditions have to be negotiated by the populations in the system's different positions. The local result is called culture. Not as something, people have, but something they do. This leads to a specific form for local social organizations, local cosmologies, and local concepts. There are therefore no universal categories, and concepts taken form one system cannot say something about the ordering or practices of another system.

Concepts are context specific. It means that local concepts

"reflect ways of living and ways of thinking characteristic of a given society,"
so that "[l]anguage and patterns of thought are interlinked" and "conceptual
systems [are] entrenched in . . . languages." (Wierzbicka 1997: 4–5, 22)

Consequently, we have to (1) untangle and eliminate Western concepts
from studies about Ancient Egypt by making these explicit, (2) establishes
the principles of the local classificatory system, and (3) relates the symbolic
system to practices (see Bergendorff 2007). No new data has been presented.
This book is based on Egyptologists own concerns about their material and
its interpretations. It is only based on accepted knowledge.

Ancient Egypt is truly a land of wonders and majestic buildings. It is so
different and extraordinary from everywhere else in the world both contemporaneously and now. Nothing to match it. One of the ancient world's seven
wonders still stand here in the form of Khufu's pyramid. It seems like a world
all to itself. Nowhere else have we seen this kind of enormous constructions,
such strange customs and such steep social hierarchies. No comparisons.

Majestic in its isolation. So many believes. There is however, no way of
turning locally produced grain into large scale "temples" and huge pyramids.
As Ekholm Friedman rightly points out, this is

to avoid the problem that surplus grain cannot be locally transformed into
bronze, cloth, palaces (of imported stone), fine jewelry, and weapons—hall-
marks of the great civilization. (Ekholm Friedman 2008: 143)

If Egypt had to rely on its own agricultural products, and the peasants
producing them, there would have been no incentive for exchange and social
hierarchy to develop. There are no incentives for unequal exchange, which is
at the root of social differentiation. This lack of incentives is known as "the
peasant enigma," referred to by Karl Marx as "the peasant sack of potatoes."

Peasant society is "formed by simple addition of homologous magnitudes,
much as potatoes in a sack form a sack of potatoes" (Lewis Feuer, ed., Marx
and Engels; From Eighteenth Brumaire of Louis Bonaparte 1852: 338). All
these similar social farming units or "potatoes in a sack" would have no
incentives to produce a surplus and start exchanging in order to create status
hierarchies.

There is no way to trick or persuade peasants so produce more than necessary. No strong leader, no charismatic person, or some kind of brave man can
change this. Authority is not the explanation. Max Weber got it wrong. No
rouse, no trickery. We would just have self-reproducing groups that would
have no incentive to produce a surplus, which is the precondition of social
hierarchies and the construction of pyramids.

Something else was going on. Emergent "kings" cannot out of thin air start to tax the local populations; you need a way to persuade people to exchange their products. You have to give them something they need in return. That would be prestige goods necessary for social reproduction. Prestige goods can never have a local origin, because then everyone would have access to them. But the coming "kings" had the means to procure these, through their monopolization of the gold deposits in the wadis leading into the Nile valley. Having these at their disposal, they could trade with the surrounding countries.

Egypt was not just one long history of cultural and material progress. It had its ups and downs. Usually called "Intermediate Periods." These periods did not happen because of tired pharaohs who ruled to long, internal fights over inheritance of the title, or excessive bureaucracy. These issues surely played a role at different points in Egypt's history. But the social conditions in Egypt closely followed the condition in the surrounding world. Egypt was part of a larger world, and this was not a static world. This surrounding world was always engaged in strategic competition over scarce resources. Egypt felt its consequences.

No matter how exotic Egypt was, it was part of a larger world. Without this surrounding world, nothing would have happened in Egypt. To become as wealthy as Egypt became and which made it possible for them to construct these huge buildings, they had to have something they could use to trade with the surrounding world. This something was gold. It made it possible for at least a section of society to import socially important prestige goods used to celebrate special social occasions.

Monopolization of this trade would paved the way for increasingly steep hierarchies. Initially we therefore find social hierarchies close to the wadis leading to gold deposits, Naqada, Hierakonpolis and Abydos. Nowhere else in Egypt did this social process take place. Eventually the monopolizing class became so extremely wealthy that they were able to muster the resources needed to build pyramids.

Divine kingship, pyramids, and so on, can all be seen as consequences of Egypt being part of a larger prestige-good system, in which Egypt traded precious metal for foreign goods that were then used as markers of status, in bride price and other *rite de passage* within Egyptian society. These prestige items passed through the elite who exchanged them "downward" in the social status hierarchy against tribute—locally produced goods, that the elite were then able to redistribute to "their subjects."

Given the right exchange rate first between local resources and foreign prestige goods and then between these and tribute from the greater populace, enormous treasures could then be amassed by the elite, and especially the "King." Who could then embark on likewise grandiose projects in all spheres of life, making him look almost, if not, divine.

Pharaohs did not like gold because they thought it was "the skin of the gods," but because it was the source of their social power and therefore they paraded in it—like gods. But "gods" were probably not an Egyptian concept. In kinship based society fortune and prestige are always linked to the workings in the ancestral world. This world is always conceptualized as a parallel and contemporaneous world. There is no hereafter or afterlife, just different forms of existence, which makes many of the concepts used to describe Egyptian understanding of dead and the death obsolete. There could not be any resurrections or rebirths.

Many Egyptologists think that the uniting of Upper and Lower Egypt was such an important event that it subsequent influenced nearly all aspects of social life in Egypt, such as in the interpretations of the Red and White crowns depicted on the head of the pharoah, his double titles, the *sed*-festival, and on the infamous Narmer Palette.

These standard notions all hinges on the idea that "The Two Lands" must represent Upper and Lower Egypt. Many Egyptologists then goes on to retracts these views, telling that the uniting was probably a drawn out process that only gradually integrated these two parts of the country. They also inform us, that both "crowns" had their origin in Upper Egypt, and that they therefore did not reflect unification. Likewise with the many double titles. These "titles" was a way of expressing the "kings" double status, and his ability to straddle the two realm of existence, as an continuously result of (the dead) Osiris siring Horus, who will become the next Osiris, who will . . . . Doubts to the meaning of the Narmer Palette has also crept in. Maybe it is just a representation of the "kings" power. But then we are left without any attempt to understand its specific message.

There are however plenty of information in both the Pyramid Texts and in the papyrus *Going Forth by Day* that also counter the standard interpretations of Egyptian practices as being about unification. After the murder of Osiris his son, Horus was made to rule the "Two Lands." This is abundantly clear. There are however no mentioning of Upper and Lower Egypt anywhere!

Horus is univocally claimed to rule the lands that the sun encircle, and it is made clear that on one hand, this is the Netherworld, so that he rules among the gods, and on the other hand, it is the Light-world, so that he rules over his human subjects. In these texts, it is also made clear that humans and gods are constituted differently. Living humans have *bas* that in "dreams" visits the realm of the "gods." When they die, their bodies are buried and their *bas* leave at daytime in the form of a bird to fly around among living people.

In contrast, "gods" are non-corporal, and their *bas* descend on human made images to enlighten these. Otherwise, they influences the lives of the living in different ways. Horus, the "king" straddles these two forms of existences being linked to Osiris in the Netherworld as his *ba*.

These issues are explored in the narrative about "genesis," in which we are introduced to the creation of the world and the births of the main "gods" and we are told how dead came into being by the murder of Osiris. Humans die, "gods" prevails. According to the main Egyptian categories, this is the difference between *neheh* and *djet*, transitory and permanence.

Then, the "crowns" can no longer be seen as representing Upper and Lower Egypt. They must be seen as graphic ways to clarify, on pictorial presentations, which role the "king" is performing, if he was acting in the Netherworld as his *ka*, or in the Light-world as Horus, the *ba* of Osiris.

Likewise, the *sed*-festival has nothing to do with unification, and the dais with the thrones back to back indicates in which realm the "king" is acting. His "ceremonious run" along the perimeter of the court is not to integrate Upper and Lower Egypt but showing that he can perform in both realms of existence.

Therefore, the Narmer Palette also is not to celebrate victory over Lower Egypt to form a united Egypt, with many casualties. On one side, Narmer is seen in a tax-collection procession that travelled around the country. To make this possible he is flying through the Gates of Horus into the chaos beyond the borders of Egypt, belonging to the Westerners. Beyond the border is the Netherworld, so on the other side of the Palette, we see Narmer's *ka* smiting the Westerners. In this way, Narmer is securing the all-important prestige goods.

Pyramids are not graves for megalomaniac pharaohs. They are the meeting ground for Re and Osiris (NN) who met in the womb of Nut as *ka* and *ba* (in the sarcophagus), placed in the Duat (grave chamber). Here they were being rejuvenated (or born again), after which they left through the Akhet (antechamber), departing the pyramid at dawn through an ascending corridor. Together they produces the continuity of cosmos, so that day follows night endlessly.

Therefore, the Egyptians could not stop building pyramids. If they stopped, the sun would not raise. At the same time Osiris' son Horus, who were for the same reason eternally made the "king" of Egypt, could no longer be "king." The "First (so-called) Intermediate Period" stopped all these contemplations about the constitution of the world and cosmos. The regional trade network simply collapsed. Byblos was ransacked, burned down, and most of the Levant was overrun by horsemen from the west and their cities abandoned. Egypt lost its most important trading partners. Ancient Egypt was for a long time left to its own devises. Many Egyptian customs felt into disuse, cultural phenomena could no longer be sustained including the divine status of the "king," which had to be revised. There were therefore no longer reasons for building pyramids.

Bibliography

Akkermans, Peter M. M. G., and Glenn M. Schwartz. 2003. *The archaeology of Syria: from complex hunter-gatherers to early urban societies (c. 16,000-300 BC)*. Cambridge: Cambridge University Press.

Algaze, Guillermo. 2014. *Ancient Mesopotamia at the dawn of civilization: the evolution of an urban landscape*. Paperback edition. Chicago: The University of Chicago Press.

Allen, James P. 1994. "Reading a Pyramid." *Hommages à jean Leclant* 1:5–28.

Allen, James P. 2015. *The ancient Egyptian pyramid texts*. Second edition. ed. *Writings from the ancient world*. Atlanta: SBL Press.

Allen, Troy D. 2009. *The ancient Egyptian family: kinship and social structure*, African studies. New York: Routledge.

Ancient Egypt—History. 2016. "*Pyramid complex of Djoser in Sakkara.*" http://www.narmer.pl/pir/dzeser_en.htm 14/08/16.

Arnold, Dieter. 1997. "Royal Cult Complexes of the Old and Middle Kingdoms." *Temples of Ancient Egypt* 75 (2):31–85.

Asaad, Tarek. 2015. "Sleep in Ancient Egypt." In *Sleep Medicine*, (eds) Chokoverty, Sudhansu&Michael Billard, p. 13–19. New York: Springer.

Aubet, Mari a Eugenia. 2013. *Commerce and colonization in the ancient Near East*. Cambridge: Cambridge University Press.

Bergendorff, Steen. 1996. *Faingu city: a modern Mekeo clan in Papua New Guinea, Lund monographs in social anthropology*. Lund, Sweden: Lund University Press.

Bergendorff, Steen. 2007. "Semantic Frameworks: Methodological Reflections on How to Understand Mekeo 'Sorcery' and 'Magic.'" *Field Methods* 19 (4):407–424.

Bergendorff, Steen. 2016. *Kinship and human evolution: making culture, becoming human*. Lanham: Lexington Books.

Crawford, Harriet E. W. 2004. *Sumer and the Sumerians*. 2nd ed. Cambridge: Cambridge University Press.

Crystalinks. 2016. "Djed." http://www.crystalinks.com/djed.html 24/11/16.

David, Rosalie. 2002. *Religion and magic in ancient Egypt*. London: Penguin.

Dodson, Aidan, and Dyan Hilton. 2004. *The complete royal families of ancient Egypt*. London: Thames & Hudson.

Encyclopædia Britannica. 2018. "Heb-Sed. Egyptian Feast." https://www.britannica.com/topic/Heb-Sed, downloaded 14/06/18.

Escobar, Arturo, and Gustavo Lins Ribeiro. 2006. *World anthropologies: disciplinary transformations within systems of power*. Oxford and New York: Berg.

Ethnography.com. 2016. "Farmer Power: The Continuing Confrontation between Subsistence Farmers and Development Bureaucrats." http://www.ethnography.com/tag/marx-bag-of-potatoes/download 20/09/20.

Faulkner, Raymond O. 2007. *The ancient Egyptian pyramid texts. Translated into English by R. O. Faulkner*. Oxford: Clarendon Press.

Faulkner, Raymond O., and Ogden Goelet. 2015. *The Egyptian book of the dead*. Twenitieth Anniversary edition. Third revised and expanded edition. San Francisco: Chronicle Books.

Frank, Andre Gunder. 1998. *ReOrient: global economy in the Asian Age*. Berkeley: University of California Press.

Frankfort, Henri. 1978 [1948]. *Kingship and the Gods. A study of ancient Near Eastern religion as the integration of society & nature. [With plates.]*. Chicago: University of Chicago Press.

Frankfort, Henri 2000 [1948]. *Ancient Egyptian Religion: an interpretation*. Dover Publication. New York.

Friedman, Jonathan. 1994. *Cultural identity and global process, Theory, culture & society*. London and Thousand Oaks, CA: Sage Publications.

Friedman, Jonathan. 2014. "Did Someone Say Globalization? The Mystification of Intellectuals and the Cunning of History." http://www.focaalblog.com/2014/07/17/did-someone-say-globalization-the-mystification-of-intellectuals-and-the-cunning-of-history-by-jonathan-friedman/ 11/01/2017.

Friedman, Kajsa Ekholm. 2008. "External Exchange and the Transformation of Central African Social Systems." *Historical Transformations: The Anthropology of Global Systems*:231-254.

History.com Editors. 2009. "Ancient Egypt." http://www.history.com/topics/ancient-history/ancient-egypt, 27/12/2016.

Jidejian, Nina. 1972. *Byblos through the ages*. [S.l.]: Dar El—Machreg, LE//Lib Orientale, LE.

Kemp, Barry J. 2018. *Ancient Egypt; anatomy of a civilization*. Third edition. London and New York: Routledge.

Kriwaczek, Paul. 2012. *Babylon: Mesopotamia and the birth of civilization*. First U.S. ed. New York: Thomas Dunne Books/St. Martin's Press.

Lankester, Francis author. 2013. *Desert boats: predynastic and pharaonic era rock-art in Egypt's central Eastern Desert : distribution, dating and interpretation*. Oxford: Archaeopress.

Leach, E. R. 1961. *Rethinking anthropology*. [S.l.]: University of London The Athlone Press.

Mark, Joshua J. 2016. "Second Dynasty of Egypt." http://www.ancient.eu/Second_Dynasty_of_Egypt/, downloaded 07/10/2016.

Mark, Joshua. J. 2018a. "The Ankh." http://www.ancient.eu/Ankh/ downloaded 23/05/18.

Mark. Joshua J. 2018b. "The Ankh." https://www.ancient.eu/Ankh/, downloaded 23/05/18.

Mark, Samuel. 1997. *From Egypt to Mesopotamia: a study of predynastic trade routes*. First ed, *Studies in nautical archaeology*. Texas A&M University Press.

Marx, K., and F. Engels. 1852. "The Eighteenth Brumaire of Louis Bonaparte 1852: 338." https://www.marxists.org/archive/marx/works/1852/18th-brumaire.

Mercer, A. B. (Translator) 2008. *"The Pyramid Texts* (Forgotten Books)." *Forgotten Books*.

Midant-Reynes, Be atrix. 2000. *The prehistory of Egypt: from the first Egyptians to the first pharaohs*. Oxford: Blackwell.

Momin, A. R. 2001. "Philosophical Anthropology in the Discourse of Sufism." *Alternative Models in Anthropology*. New Delhi: Indira Gandhi National Centre for the Arts.

O'Connor, David. 1991. "Boat Graves and Pyramid Origins: New Discoveries at Abydos, Egypt." *Expedition* 33 (3):5.

O'Connor, David B., and Andrew Reid. 1990. *Ancient Egypt in Africa*. Routledge: London and New York.

Pharaoh se. 2018. "The Royal Canon of Turin." https://pharaoh.se/turin-papyrus-king-list, downloaded 31/01/2018.

Pierre, Tallet, and Marouard Gregory. 2014. "THE HARBOR OF KHUFU on the Red Sea Coast at Wadi al-Jarf, Egypt." *Near Eastern Archaeology* 77 (1):4–14. doi: 10.5615/neareastarch.77.1.0004.

Pinch, Geraldine. 2004. *Egyptian mythology: a guide to the gods, goddesses, and traditions of ancient Egypt*. New York and Oxford: Oxford University Press.

Pinch, Geraldine. 2006. *Magic in ancient Egypt*. Rev. and updated ed. London: British Museum Press.

Raffaele, Francesco. 2003. "Late Predynastic and Early Dynastic Egypt." http://xoomer.virgilio.it/francescoraf/, downloaded 18/07/2018.

Rankine, David. 2006. *HEKA: the practices of ancient Egyptian ritual and magic*. London: Avalonia.

Saraswati, Baidyanath. 2001. "Alternative Paradigms in Anthropology: The Cosmic Anthropological Principle." *The nature of man and culture. Alternative paradigms in anthropology*. New Delhi: Aryan Books International.

Shaw, Ian. 2000. *Egypt and the outside world*. Oxford: Oxford University Press.

Shinnie, P. L. 1996. *Ancient Nubia*. London: Kegan Paul International.

Silverman, David P. 1997. *Ancient Egypt*. London: Piatkus.

Spalinger, Anthony. 2013. "The Organisation of the Pharaonic Army (Old to New Kingdom)." In *Ancient Egyptian administration*, 393–478. Brill.

Tambiah, Stanley Jeyaraja. 1990. *Magic, science, religion, and the scope of rationality*. Cambridge: Cambridge University Press.

Teeter, Emily. 2011. *Religion and ritual in ancient Egypt*. Cambridge and New York: Cambridge University Press.

The Ancient Egypt Site. 2014. Royal Titulary. http://www.ancient-egypt.org/language/royal-titulary.html, downloaded 30/06/17.

The Mystery of Sekhemkhet's Pyramid. 2016. http://www.catchpenny.org/sekhem. html 17/08/16.

Tour Egypt. 2016a. "Egypt: Khasekhem/Khasekhemwy of Egypt's 2nd Dynasty." http://www.touregypt.net/featurestories/khasekhem.htm 12/10/2016.

Tour Egypt. 2016b. "Egypt: Khasekhem/Khasekhemwy of Egypt's 2nd Dynasty." http://www.touregypt.net/featurestories/khasekhem.htm 12/10/2016.

Tyldesley, Joyce A. 2003. *Pyramids: the real story behind Egypt's most ancient monuments*. London: Viking.

Tyldesley, Joyce A. 2011. *Myths & legends of Ancient Egypt*. London: Penguin.

Verner, Miroslav. 2002. *The pyramids: their archaeology and histroy [i.e. history]*. London: Atlantic Books.

Vendel, O. 2016a. "Egyptian History dynasties 3-5." http://www.nemo.nu/ibisportal/ 0egyptintro/3egypt/index.htm, downloaded 21/11/2016.

Vendel O. 2016b. "Egyptian History dynasties 3-5." http://www.nemo.nu/ibisportal/ 0egyptintro/3egypt/index.htm, 30/11/2016.

Vendel, O. 2016c. "Egyptian History dynasties 3-5." http://www.nemo.nu/ibisportal/ 0egyptintro/3egypt/index.htm, 01/12/2016.

Vendel, O. 2016d. "Egyptian History dynasties 6-1." http://www.nemo.nu/ibisportal/ 0egyptintro/4egypt/index.htm, 10/12/2016.

Wallerstein, Immanuel Maurice. 1974. *The modern world-system, Studies in social discontinuity*. New York: Academic Press.

Wenke, Robert J. 2009. *The ancient Egyptian state: the origins of Egyptian culture (c. 8000-2000 BC), Case studies in early societies*. Cambridge, UK and New York: Cambridge University Press.

Wilkinson, Toby A. H. 2003. *Genesis of the Pharaohs: dramatic new discoveries that rewrite the origins of ancient Egypt*. London: Thames & Hudson.

Woolley, Leonard. 1928 [1965]. *The Sumerians*. Oxford: Clarendon Press.

Woolley, Leonard. 1963. *Excavations at Ur: a record of twelve years' work*. 1st ed.!, fourth impression. Benn: Barnes & Noble.

Zettler, Richard L., and Lee Horne. 1998. *Treasures from the royal tombs of Ur*. Philadelphia and Great Britain: University of Pennsylvania, Museum of Archaeology and Anthropology.

Index

About the Author

Steen Bergendorff has a PhD in anthropology from University of Copenhagen, Denmark, and a doctorate from Lunds University, Sweden. He has worked both at the Department of Anthropology in Copenhagen and at International Development Studies at Roskilde University. He has done extensive fieldwork in Papua New Guinea providing him with profound insight into kinship, personhood, and mythology. His main interest is in historical anthropology and world-system theory. These interests has now turned into a keen interest in the historical and social foundation of Ancient Egypt. Some of his main publications include *Faingu City—A Modern Mekeo Clan, Simple lives; Cultural Complexity—Rethinking Culture in Terms of Complexity Theory, Kinship and Human Evolution—Making Culture Becoming Human*, and "Contextual Translations—Concepts and Practices among the Mekeo o Papua New Guinea" (2009).

www.ingramcontent.com/pod-product-compliance
Lightning Source LLC
Chambersburg PA
CBHW022322280326
41932CB00010B/1191

9 781793 610065